THE MURAL OF WAKEFUL SLEEP

BOOKS BY LAURENCE LIEBERMAN

POETRY

The Mural of Wakeful Sleep
(1985)

Eros at the World Kite Pageant
(1983)

God's Measurements
(1980)

The Osprey Suicides
(1973)

The Unblinding
(1968)

CRITICISM

*Unassigned Frequencies:
American Poetry in Review*
(1977)

The Achievement of James Dickey
(1968)

THE MURAL OF WAKEFUL SLEEP

by

Laurence Lieberman

COLLIER BOOKS
Macmillan Publishing Company
NEW YORK
COLLIER MACMILLAN PUBLISHERS
LONDON

Copyright © 1985 by Laurence Lieberman

All rights reserved. No part of this book may be reproduced or transmitted in any form or by any means, electronic or mechanical, including photocopying, recording or by any information storage and retrieval system, without permission in writing from the Publisher.

Macmillan Publishing Company
866 Third Avenue, New York, N.Y. 10022
Collier Macmillan Canada, Inc.

Library of Congress Cataloging in Publication Data

Lieberman, Laurence.
    The mural of wakeful sleep.

  I. Title.
PS3562.I43M8   1985b   811′.54   84-27435
ISBN 0-02-069780-5

10 9 8 7 6 5 4 3 2 1

Printed in the United States of America

The Mural of Wakeful Sleep is also published in a hardcover edition by Macmillan Publishing Company.

For Anita Lieberman

Acknowledgments

I wish to thank the editors of the following magazines, in which these poems first appeared:

American Poetry Review: "The Organist's Black Carnation"
"The Queen's Last Fittings"
"The Banana Madonna"
"The Mural of Wakeful Sleep"
"The Architect Monk"

The Carrell: "Eighty-Six Nassau Bay Baptizings"
"Parlor Ship Gallery"

Chariton Review: "The Telephone Piracies"

The Hudson Review: "Queen of the Billiards"
"Dominoes and Politics on the Morne"

The Kenyon Review: "The Dungeon Amorist"

Memphis State Review: "Heartshot: One Page from the Cannoneer's Journal"

Michigan Quarterly Review: "The Dominican Coachman"

The Nation: "Siesta"
"The Banana Dwarf" (also in *Anthology of Magazine Verse*, 1985 Edition, Beverly Hills: Monitor Book Company)

Partisan Review: "Slave Platoons Gouging the Capitol"

The Reaper: "Sunday: My Throat Afire"

Sewanee Review: "Woman's Tongue"

The South Carolina Review: "Fairchild Market: Meats and Mauby"
"Cane Fires"

Tar River Poetry: "Jamaica Flambeaux"

Contents

I. JAMAICA AND THE DOMINICAN REPUBLIC / 1

    The Dominican Coachman / 3
    The Banana Dwarf / 5
    Siesta / 8
    Jamaica Flambeaux / 10
        I. *Crab Hunters* / 10
        II. *Demolitions Crew* / 12

II. THE BAHAMAS / 15

    The Organist's Black Carnation / 17
    Two Nassau Mirages / 21
        I. *Slave Platoons Gouging the Capitol* / 21
        II. *Rock Galleon of the Foothills* / 23
    Eighty-Six Nassau Bay Baptizings / 25
    The Architect Monk / 29
    Heartshot: One Page from the Cannoneer's Journal / 31
    The Dungeon Amorist / 37

III. BARBADOS / 43

    Woman's Tongue / 45
    The Telephone Piracies / 49
    Cane Fires / 57
    Fairchild Market: Meats and Mauby / 61
    Barbados Drought Songs / 66
        I. *Menopause of the Cowherds* / 66
        II. *A Frieze of Sheep* / 68

IV. ST. LUCIA / 71

    Queen of the Billiards / 73
    Dominoes and Politics on the Morne / 76
    Sunday: My Throat Afire / 82
    Parlor Ship Gallery / 86
    The Queen's Last Fittings / 88
    The Banana Madonna / 92

V. THE MURAL OF WAKEFUL SLEEP / 95

I. Jamaica and the Dominican Republic

THE DOMINICAN COACHMAN

    ALL THIRTEEN CHILDREN—oh, by three or four
    mothers—live in New York.
    Upwards of thirty grandkids, at last tally.
Well, no, he doesn't
miss them

       too much—they all write letters. But oh,
    too many! "Too many kids,
    kids' kids, or letters?" I ask. No answer.
Yet shakes his head.
The mind

       spins with the numbers, dizzying numbers.
    Best to not count, not add up—
    except wives, mistresses, concubines....
No lose count there!
How well

       he relishes the unique niceties of each
    chattel in his scattered
    harem. In his mid-Seventies' heyday,
four paramours live
at far ends

       of town, none too near. Piloting the horse cart,
    once a highborn calling, today's
    a dying art; while he, forty years' veteran,
keeps up his lifelong
ardor

       for the historic enterprise.... A one-time
    New York subway token
    monitor. Two years in Manhattan. Three
years, each, in The Bronx
and Queens.

       Seven years' exile, *bastante*! Back home to stay
    now, Santiago birth-
    place never so dear as these last

ten years of ferrying
townsfolk

 and tourists, alike, in the fourwheeler
around parks and plazas.
New York *ees loco,* too much hurry,
long hours, much rent,
muy frio.

 Santiago's quiet. In work, in play, the Spirit
sleeps, wakes, at its own sweet
will.... "But what about the guns?" I ask,
two squads of four
militia

 each, straggling past in either direction,
looking heavy-bored. Dazed.
Dangerous ennui. The percussive march
step, half-muffled, half-
audible,

 persists in their off-duty minstrel-jokey
gait. *Ah, Good Samaritans*
(so saith our Coachman, his greetings
smiled, gladeyed), packing
rifles,

 cartridge belts jampacked—swelled for sport,
only! *Ah, campadre, good*
buddies. See how they wave, to friends,
to *gringos.* All one happy
family!

THE BANANA DWARF

I TURN THE MARKET CORNER, then peer down
the busiest Santo
Domingo
central thoroughfare,
sidewalk traffic as thronged
with surplus foot peddlers and shoppers
as the vehicular jam-up
on the mainstreet intersection. The number
of side-by-side lanes,
in road *or* walkway, varies
from three to ten:
pedestrians, buglike motorcarts, bikes
and cabs whirl and slither around each other,

weave in and out of formation, like couples
on a disco-clogged
dance floor. . . .
At a city block corner,
three roads distant, I see—
gliding swiftly through a thick huddle of heads
and shoulders—a whirring machine!
Is it a crane, two blurred yellow derrick beams
swung on each side
of the advancing figure
or apparatus—
but not mowing down the crush of bodies
it plows across? The heads bob this way and that,

steering clear of those thick yellow posts
hoisting burdens, two
on each side,
revealed to be tall stalks
of bananas—a pair suspended
from each long wooden pole. The banana dwarf
takes springy strides, so much bounce
in pads of his moccasins, he matches a gymnast
on a trampoline;

for length and limber play,
his transverse rods
resemble pole vaulters' posts. Amazingly,
no single bananas fly loose—the ripest clusters,

even, stay intact—his difficult balancement
both dance step and juggler's
lofty art.
This spry, red-cheeked midget
looms tall, tall—and oh!—still taller
for the yellow tiered forest of fruit he wields
with his graceful plump shoulders,
his back and neck muscles rippling. The taut fruit
of his flesh: cords
and sinews, sleek flexors bunched
under his skin—
bananas themselves—bulge the human rind
of his upper torso.... He sways nearer and nearer.

Though I walk jauntily toward him, I seem
to stand still, to hang
in a pool
of banana fluff, banana
yellow light emitted from the stalks:
a cloud, in which I float, weightless, tongueless,
wanting to speak—to beg a choice
ripe banana to eat! *He flies. He sings the all-*
saving nutrients,
blessings of the Banana
God. He plucks
a sample banana here, a sample there, peels
one, offers a munch to each of several passersby,

drops a pinch of banana in my outstretched
palm. *His bare chest, shoulders,*
shed their skins.
That ripply musculature,
bared and exposed, offers itself up
to the eyes of one and all, to the great yellow
Eye of the Banana Lord, Sun.

And when he glides behind me, my Dominican
pesos flicker
like a new papery tongue
between his teeth,
the extra money bisecting his widest smile,
a nine-banana spiral draped over my wrist, the coil

and whorl of the golden cluster symmetrical
as a pineapple, my small vine-
twist of fruit
wee replica of the many-tiered,
many-wreathed stalks of banana garlands
slung from the Banana Apostle's shoulders. . . . All those
he passes—ladies of wide girth,
men of tall stature, children—must duck, weave, swerve,
but not one Soul
collides with a single gold
shaft! Their moves
guided by his hops, they dodge banana flower-burst,
their dance in traffic as deft as his fleet pirouettes!

SIESTA

No rustle.
    Not a lip
        stirs in the town square,
        the park frozen
in mid-Siesta... The horse-drawn buggies
are parked in roadside stalls, their drivers curled
        in front seat corners
           like snails; long horse necks drooped
between traces,
    in stupor, or
        quiet munchings of hay.
        Thick manes wag
in the breeze, while snuffles punctuate
the masters' snores: a mixed chorus of sleep drone
        and gap-toothed slow hay
           mastications... The buses, fire engines,
ambulancias,
    and tractors—
        all parked at odd angles—
        straddle lanes
half-on, half-off the highway. Dormant
at the foot of park statues (military sculptures:
        pistols aimed, swords
           drawn, or crouched beside cannons),
the hodgepodge
    fleet of trucks lies
        sprawled. They strike poses
        of slain dragons
or disabled war tanks: front or rear axle
swung over low hedge, one wheel propped on high curb,
        or athwart boulder;
        whole garbage truck-back chassis
atilt. Cement
    truck's bumper
        near-submerged in the park
        fountain. Loaded

banana trailer and sugar-cane trailer
sandwich the cab of giant diesel semi (its three-
      story-high fortress
         towering over the sunburst

cornucopias
    of fruit and cane),
        dislodged from its massive
        chrome-silver
torpedo: close facsimile of an Inter-
Continental Ballistic Missile! The twenty-four-wheel
        oil rig tanker
          floats in a field opposite

the plaza square...
    Many drivers' doors—
        above, below—slant ajar:
        a few doors,
swivelling on their hinges, gently sway
in the wind; others anchored by legs poking upwards
        through windows, feet
          shoeless, sock-bedraggled or bare....

JAMAICA FLAMBEAUX

I. Crab Hunters

Twilight, that fast-change artist, shimmers twenty
swift color jumps from rose to maroon,
each curve in the road streaking into skyscapes
a pastel shade
      duskier in the palette
of blackening purples. A one minute switchback inland, dimmed
      by wooded foothills—we reconnoiter

      back to shore: all color is sunk in murk of grays. . . .
The many couples lap-piled in rear seats,
      chug-a-lugging gallons of rumpunch, ignore scattered
heaps in low brush,
      others looming on the pavement
ahead (droppings of a rockslide?); fearing avalanche of cliff
      debris, I motion to stomp on the brakes,

      shouting *whoa, whoa*! But the van driver laughs, steady
on the throttle, unslowing. He elbows me
in the ribs. Three larger hunks, spaced in a row
near the road edge,
      rise at once—they levitate,
a foot or more. Suspended by invisible cables from above?
      No! I see tinkertoy stick-legs, frail

      as pipecleaners, propped under the ovoid shapes.
One lowers at our approach. The others
      swoop into roadside thickets, two bright dots flashing
in our dim headlamps.
      Beads of eyes on stalks—crabs!
Dozens, here and there, in clumps of three to six. Standing fixed
      as if frozen in place, one moment

      (waving a single gleamy claw, perhaps); racing
on stilts, the next. Many droves of crabs,
      sprung from nests or sanctuary at dusk. Three children,

    idling in a horse-
        drawn carriage, approach; for these,
we brake, slowing to a halt—the doddering nag (a bony hulk)
        straddling the center line. Waving lit

        wands, the children plunge into tall grass at roadside,
        wooden buckets slung from their shoulders
    on straps. They wade and rummage through marshy sawgrass.
The flares, like mammoth
        fireflies, dart in zigzag paths;
or halt, bobbing in place, while the scouts plunder crabs, crabs,
        filling the deep tubs—many times over—

        with the evening's haul. . . We resume our cruising speed.
        For miles down the road, we catch glimmers
    of flares upraised, flares lowered to the ground, threading
through leafy scrub.
        The hour of the crab hunt peaks, lights
of the chase eight or ten thick in a single roadside acre; then,
        the road clears of shells. All lights pale. . . .

II. Demolitions Crew

      Our van whipped by gusts, we ascend a high overpass,
        the frame-metal bridge spanning Great River,
          widest of six rivers on our route. Halfway across
the rattly plank floor,
          we sight a spectacle below, and park.
Beside the bridge's pylon, another light show is in progress.
          Three ghostly figures float in high-piled

          girders, climbing makeshift ladder rungs of towers
        sloped amid steel beams and crossbeams
          bunched in a heap. Helmeted and masked, they wave
heavy implements
          spitting light. Ah!—no *crabs* roost
in that maze of spires. The steeplejacks clamp their waists
        to center posts. Each, aiming a stream

          of fire at nearby metal bars, heats the targets
        from pink to white hot glows with blowtorch,
          and slams the molten poles with a wide flat hammer—
snapping thick rods
          with single hammerblows. Soon,
two or three bulky segments of warped steel grillework, severed
        from the frame, drop, clanging as they fall—

          tier by tier—to the shore below... One tall crewman,
        lowering himself arm over arm
          from a rope sling device, dives, spinning, fifty feet
from the uppermost
          girders. He enters the low cab cage
(a gigantic crab shell?) of a great towering crane, half-hidden
        in shadows behind the dishevelled

          steel skeleton. The crane advances, tanklike,
        on runners—deeply plowing the beach,
          leaving furrowed tracks in its wake. The cab operator,
swinging the forged-
          iron vast hook, snares and lifts

each of those fallen, mangled chunks of metal and drops them,
    one by one, into the deep bin

      of a truck semi-rig. . . . *Above, rows of fire spewn*
      from torchgun barrels! Hot steel-joints,
    whitely aglow! New constellations in a thick-starred
night, the civic foreman's
    acetylene comets and meteors
ignite the gaps between galaxies of stars and planets, blazing
    for brief moments, then dying out. . . .

II. The Bahamas

THE ORGANIST'S BLACK CARNATION

ODD MUSIC,
cutting through horn blasts and squawks of traffic, asserts
        its live and public wash
    of sound rolling in waves across the town square. . . . Christ Church
      Cathedral. Once in the Church rear courtyard, we find
    we can disencumber the river of organ song from percussive
        street blare—
      its source, the deep hall within tall double doors,
        unbolted. Mother
                and I, goose-stepping
    on circular, wide ceramic tiles of the walkway, traverse
      the Church
    gardens, and pass through the side entrance. The instrument,
      itself, so near the door, we almost collide
with the seated performer, his arms and legs all pumping
      together, the four limbs
utterly weightless, his moves between upper and lower keyboards
effortless, unwilled,

as buoyed up
by a hidden well of pure feeling as his side-to-side runs
      across any one keyboard.
    Tall. Blond. Bearded. American. Stops to turn pages. Smiles
      Hello. *Any music you prefer,* he asks? *Oh yes,
    any Bach*. Bach Preludes unfold, at once—the music open
      before him.
      But he could be playing from memory. Or sightreading.
        A little of each,
                I'd guess, never up close
    to an organist expert before, I gasp at agilities
      of legwork,
    the sheer quantity of wooden pedals, joined in a concave arc
      recessed below his legs, his knees spreading wide,
    wider, as he reaches for the pedals at either far end—
      there are so many
moving parts, keys and pedals above and below, I can see, at last,
why organ solo

music I've heard
can sound like a whole orchestra of virtuosos. How lightly
          he taps the keys, oceans
     of rich basses circulating around the whole chapel, cloister,
          and outer chambers—the tall pipes widely distributed
     throughout the walls, as if the entire church is the vehicle
          and body
     of the instrument, the keyboards and pedal valves
          a mere touch control
                              relay. . . Organ melody
     outside the church, diffused, half-muffled by traffic,
          is carried
     afar, and, for moments, rushes close to the distant listener's
          ears; but withindoors, the whole church interior
     is charged with the music's amplified wave pulsings, notes
          that seem to pass beyond
all time limits, as in Bruckner's symphonies. It's all a breathing,
influx and efflux

of lungs shaped
like tall pipes, the wide oval pipe tops releasing blent voices,
          four voice octaves rolled
     into the one chorale. . . . He chats with us now as he plays, simpler
          passages he *must* know from memory. Keeps turning pages,
     though. No mistakes. His movements all dancelike. I look and look,
          scrutinize
     his hands, the faraway pipes, for clues to the miracle
          of lightness of touch—
                              so feathery his patter
     of the keys. Now the church walls seem to shudder,
          the pipe mouths
     recoiling upon the seeming pantomime of his performance,
          a magic dumbshow of silently flicking the keys
     with velvet-soft fingertips. And there is no way I can fathom
          the hairlinefine exchanges
between his ten fingers' prowl of three keyboards and those distant
tall pipe-groanings,

pipe-wailings. . . .
We'll embark, today, on our mother-son, off-the-beaten-path

                    Island treks. So we attend
          to his genial warnings. The bars are all dangerous. But back
            in the ghettoes—*we call it Over the Hill*—the risk
       of muggings, or worse, is critical. In broad day light. Chamber-of-Commerce
             won't hear of it, but, night or day, no hill or backwoods
                  sector is safe! Then,
                              why has *he* stayed on
           these six months, braced for still another six, grit
                and pluck
       stamped on the cast of his jaw, his tall slender profile,
            orange-freckled face, neck and arm. Now he stands,
       for a moment, flashing his smile in the lit column of dust motes
                whirling in a pool of sun
that pours through the skylight. He signals the three black nuns
in the chapel doorway

to step back!
So doing, their twenty-odd local charges (boys and girls
                in equal numbers: ages
       five to nine, say) come racing to the organ bench. He resumes,
            playing his own transcriptions of nursery songs,
         Christmas carols, a few native Island hymns—the children singing
                out of tune,
            getting the words wrong, no two in sync, but all
                finding another home
                                  to inhabit in the piped
            lullabies and jingles. Two forward children squat
                on the floor
       near his feet, staying just clear of those pumping knees,
            intrigued by his undulations—the split second
       reflexes of his feet floating over the pedals. A round-faced
                petite girl clambers
upon the organ cabinet, and sits, cross-legged, alongside
keyboards, memorizing

taps of his keys
beneath her legs. Two boys squeeze next to him, on opposite
              ends of the bench; while many
         form a ring around his seat, arms on each other's shoulders.

        He sings with them, not to lead the tunes, but more
    to tag along. The churchwomen scowl, from time to time—threaten
        to send away
      the few least controlled kids, but he calms them all
         with his *Hush, now!* (finger
                  to his lips). The children,
    asway, appear to dance from the hips, their legs bobbing
      in place. . . . *I*
see two dozen blackbirds, or ravens, perched on his shoulders,
    his balding scalp, weightless, hopping on jointed-twig
legs across his redhaired curly forearms, alighting on his knees,
      his wrists. And one blackbird
lands on the tip of his nose, both perfectly still. Now it's
a black butterfly.

Those soft wings,
flapping, turn to petals of a black carnation, which falls
      to his shirt lapel. . . . I waken
    from a standup daydream, a bird romance, the blond organist
      still playing singalong tunes—the kids humming offkey,
   while they follow their holy guides, public maidservants (in God)
      to the school
    van parked in the rear, their short midday recess
        come to a close. . . . He fears
              he's losing his touch
   at the organ knows he may well fail his instrumental
      M. A. exam
   when he sails back home to Seattle it's been such a hot summer
      can't practise when he perspires so much for weeks
    he's been soaking in his own stale body foetors. . . . No less
      absorbed in his Bach scores,
for carrying on two conversations with mother, with me—he blossoms
musical feast for us. . . .

TWO NASSAU MIRAGES

I. Slave Platoons Gouging the Capitol

      Our van glides
        up a cobblestone road—
        particolored, the mild grade
      deadended in a paved bubble: this cul-de-sac opens
         into a steep flight of stairs,
      66 white tall steps of *The Queen's Staircase* agleam,
   rising to the crag,
where hills of solid rock house
   the Capitol...

        Far right, looms
          the Governor's Mansion, hewn
          out of stone cliffs by slave hundreds
      in chain gangs, who wielded their one tool, the *driell*.
        A chopper. A rock-hacking scythe.
     The axelike curved blades, two-edged, flung to either side
    of the wooden shafts
like jaws of a hammerhead shark, flash
   in the midday

         sun.... *We see,*
        again: hundreds of menials
       linked by metal leg cuffs, thick anklets,
     strung out in long teams, so little space between toilers
       their swings nearly graze the bare calves
     of the next in line; but the rhythm of hillside progress—
   a tromp and trudge
in lockstep paced by the tom-toms—is
   a precision dance:

        no missteps,
        no slips of the swung blades,
       as the workforce wends its clockwise
      course over Government Hill's rocky face.... We conjure,
       today, the grim morning platoons,
     some eight or nine rows at once, one rotating tier of hoop-

  backed rock crushers
stationed over the other, so many
  ant colony

    lineups circling
   conic earth mounds. The pattern
   of travail—ceaseless, unfluctuant—
  commences in first light, or predawn glimmers: bobbing heads,
   sharp elbows, bony half-clad hips
    fading in mists, fog pockets. . . . Now smoke trails white out
  three black figures
(typewriter errors painted over
  with *liquid*

    paper), the next
   two men in line perfectly intact;
   on the terrace below, a lean headless
  torso leads a legless muscly physique, the missing parts
   of some figures matching up with
  amputations of near, or distant, tier mates. The witness's
eye assembles
far-flung body quarters, stray limbs,
  into composite

    wholes: anatomies
   glimpsed through slow-thinning smoke
   puffs, rising ground fogs. . . . If one trips
  and falls from the ledge, the whole row may follow, dragged
    down the hill face: one chain-rank,
  collapsing on another, could trigger an all-but-unstoppable
roller flux. . .
Free-falling bodies. . . An avalanche
  of mortals. . . .

II. Rock Galleon of the Foothills

Sighting ninety
    degrees sheer left,
        and above Government House
        in the nearer
distance, we track a long keel in the sea
of sky—cleaving low fog banks curled like cotton
        bales.... *Specters*
        are hatched like contagious bacilli

in this haze.
    Lingering spools
        of mist shroud rock balcony
        here, stone pillars,
smokestacks and rope ladders there. We scan
the marbly jutting hull from bow to stern: gunnels
        topped by ramparts,
        toothed stone parapets; shipsides

disguised, oddly,
    as castle walls,
        grooved and notched with windows—
        shuttered portholes,
misshaped, squarely, in high rectangular
blocks? Shipmates, climbing the tall aerial masts,
        pat the mainsheet
        and small yardarm of sail... But no!

The wide mainsail,
    aflutter in wind,
        is the Bahamian Sovereignty's
        flag; the fake
mainmast a flag pole; the cloudlike sky surf—
submerging two thirds of the deep hull—*is* cloud;
        the slow-motion
        breakers and swells *are* low heaps

of cumulo-stratus;
    the gay skipper

    who waves hello to our troop,
     perched upright
in the tower balcony, no Flying Dutchman,
but a mere Minister of Finance taking time out
      from his Spartan
      bankers' hours to hail visitors. . . .

Driving uphill
  behind the lofty stern
    of white stucco, we are blinded
     on the curves—
submerged for moments, awash in the ship's
smoky dense wake. Crossing the drawbridge, we hear
     a quick drumroll,
      thunder of rickety planks. We brake,

screech to a halt,
  bumper just inches
    from the guardrail. . . . Ghost ship,
     aloft—poised
over the Capitol Building—is Fort Finn
Castle, architected in the shape of a warboat;
     whether to dizzy
      and befuddle approaching enemy

battleships,
  or to play tricks
    on thousands of fool voyagers'
     gullible eyes—
we tourists of future centuries. . . . *This rock*
galleon of the foothills, great stone ark landlocked,
     forever anchored
      to cliffs. Oh one true Ship of State!

EIGHTY-SIX NASSAU BAY BAPTIZINGS

     IDLING SHOREWARD,
    we reach the highest point of roadside
uphill from those thousands
    of Baptists who converge—
from three directions—
upon the roped-off long stretch of inshore waters.
    The ropes border a ten-foot-wide
strip of bay inlet extending for the length, say,
of an Olympicsized
    swimming pool. "Let's stop here?" I ask,
    "for the balcony birds-eye view
of the whole Baptist

     assemblage." "What,
    and miss the baby dunkings? Mystical
rush!" you reply. "See water
    splash, when heads are submerged
and upraised. Catch
some spray on your camera lens in the wet crossfire.
    Better still, you a verse writer,
be Baptized, yourself. *Himself he sung,* your first
poet, didn't he say?
    Yourself be dunked, or doused—be inside,
    part and parcel, our tenth annual
Baptism rites!"

    No newshawk, I bid
    him walk ahead, his crack newsteam
plus clunky TV equipment
    trailing behind, while I stay
on the sidelines,
poised for the full panorama of a dozen, or more,
    brass bands decked in tricolored
uniforms, performing as they march. Each follows
its own drummers' beat,
    though all slowly migrate toward a beach
    starting gate. First installments
of Baptizees—

                    ranging from wizened
              folks in their nineties to babies
         clasped in their mother's arms—
                    wait their place in single file
         long lines, each cloaked
         in their church's white gowns, lace trim varied
                    from sect to sect. . . . Sunday. High
         Noon. At last count, some eighty-six new members
         of the faith await wettings.
                    Some sixteen islands are represented
              by one or more novitiates,
and most land strips

                    (even small islets,
              whose sole pilgrim wayfarer graces
         this season's lineup) mobilized
                    their own brass bands from grass-
         roots local tooters
         to blare fanfares for their instant home celebrants.
                    Each band makes its color-coded
         pitch for its own Church parish; and to my uphill
         vantage, the many trains
                    of walkers, wobbly processions, appear
              to fork into the Baptist sector
of roped-off beach

                    like crooked spokes
              radiating from the hub of a wheel,
         so many separate platoons
                    of arriving kinsfolk, I lose
         sight of blacktop
         roads from town, then dirt roads from hills inland,
                    as well. Now all the crowd halts,
         bunched in one great puffy, toadstoolshaped knot:
         the various brass bands'
                    group colors stand out, here and there,
              like flower displays highlighted
upon a field backdrop

                    of grays, austere
              colors worn by most parishioners

                for the occasion's sanctity....
                        Two frock-coated Deans of a Church
                federation raise
                their hands for silence, make announcements I can't
                        decipher at this distance. One hand
        makes a sweeping gesture, a signal to all musicians
        to start playing a brass
                overture to the awesome ceremony, soon
                to begin—no chance for prior
marathon rehearsal:

                the vast scattered
                        assemblage of trumpets, horns, tubas
                and drums stay in perfect accord,
                        hardly a note straying from unison
        of this sprawled
        ensemble. The taller of the two High Priests steps
                to the front of the line of white-
        gowned baptismal supplicants, lifts a frail brown
        liver-spotted arm and joins
                hands of this woman (the most ancient
                human I've ever beheld upright,
by her own sinews)

                with a mother holding
                a days-old infant wrapped in a white
        thick bundle. The elder, announced—
                by megaphone blasts—to be the oldest
        person to receive
        Baptism rites in Nassau's history, is one hundred three
                years old; and she agrees to submit
        to dunking with the tiny baby in her arms (six days
        old, perhaps), the marriage
                of youth and age. Just-born and soon-to-die.
                This is not a quaint local custom,
but a spontaneous—

                if symbolic—yoking
                by the clergyman, who has a keen eye
        for good theatre: he knows how
                to send a thrill up the spines

             of Church devotees
                of all ages. Now the pastor, chanting into the megaphone,
                      recites apt Scripture for this year's
              surprise bonanza. The baby's mother, fearful at first
              to relinquish her grasp
                    of the squalling tot, relents: her face bliss—
                 her babe the One chosen, after all,
    to lead the processional. . . .

THE ARCHITECT MONK

    THE WHOLE NATION, some seven hundred scattered
  dots and free form
  mobile cutouts of land, strewn over
a six-hundred-mile
wide arc

    of Caribbean Sea.... In these flat isles, we
  are impressed by low
  heights: a hillock titled *Mountain,*
the tall white water
tower

    of Nassau a local skyscraper. The monk,
  stricken with a mild
  rage for altitude, chose Cat Island's
Como Hill—two hundred
fifty feet

    at the peak—for his first monastery:
  himself sole architect
  and builder, the job of ten years'
fitting board on board,
aided

    by primitive tools only. And basic manual
  homecrafts... The last nail
  struck, the last bucket of mortar
emptied, its contents
hardened

    between the misshapen loaves of rough stone
  he'd chiseled and cut
  from the sandstone steep butte flanking
the cliff's west rim. Yes,
ten years'

    disavowal of speech, no word spoken
  but in chaste society
  of shore birds, led him to rescind aiders—

  he the lone quarry
gouger,

    he the stone mason, stained-glass-smith, steel
  smelter, roof shingler.
  He propped the roof's welded zinc A-frame
on a colossal sawhorse
apparatus. . . .

    His first hermitage overtops any lighthouse
  or high watchtower
  in the sickle-curved sweep of isles. Today
a migrant contractor
of chapels,

    tabernacles, bell towers, and mission
  quarters, he lays
  biennial cornerstones, and erects
a colony of two dozen
churches

    on sites rotated over five islands, the last
  St. Augustine's Monastery
  in Nassau, capped with a science lab
and planetarium's mosquelike
bubble dome. . . .

HEARTSHOT: ONE PAGE
FROM THE CANNONEER'S JOURNAL

I.

So here,
on the flat edge of this mesa overhang, the great mammoth
    castiron kettle
  was bonfired to a boil; the super-heated metal balls
    dexterously lifted, steaming, from the bubbly
  cauldron with huge steel tongs. Two sergeants of artillery
    hoisted
    each arm of the clamps, the thick cannonballs, ablaze,
      held, one by one,

in tong
jaws, then suspended directly in the flames, just touching
    the hottest live coals.
  Their faces swathed in canvas masks, their hands and forearms
    insulated with coarse burlap gloves (precursor
  to modern firefighters' asbestos), they lifted the molten spheres,
    white-hot
    on one side, luminous, and dropped them in the maws
      of upturned cannon

barrels
pre-aimed at the distant square rigged French battle galleons,
    while a third officer
  touched a flaming torch to the short tow or hemp fuses,
    instantly combustible, four squat side-by-side
  cannons' powder kegs ignited at once, perhaps, the first shots
    at gunboats,
    the approaching three-or-four-masted frigates flanked
      by caravels, swift fleet

of backups
(a preemptive strike!), wrenching the element of surprise
    from Napoleon's secret
  twilight strike force—thanks to the early warning system
    of downisland sentries. Lookouts on remote

        unpopulated atolls. Harbingers' oar-driven speedboats carried
            the message,
          skilled to exploit to advantage every trick shift
            of the trade winds.

Single-mast
cutters took clever tacks around shady windbreak, hugged
        secluded coast hill
    ranges, and vanished into hidden tunnel underpass
        bucking heady currents—their skippers armed
    with hand-me-down mapped waterway secrets of many local
        fisherfolk
        generations. The pre-dawn beamed SOSs of sloop
        couriers burst upon

the moonlit
glitter of Nassau's harbor! Flares waved. Exchange of signals
        from guardboats to coastal
    watchtowers. The sea scouts, veteran oarsmen, two dozen
        furlongs from shore—yet the primitive semaphor
    code warnings delivered. Starry-skied hours lead time to spare. . . .
        Hot shots.
        Heartshot. Four well-aimed jumbo cannons detonate
        their powder charges

in rat-
a-tat-tat succession. Four fireballs flash once at the barrel
        mouths. Vanish. Vaguely streak
    like near-fizzled meteorites, swift-faded shooting stars,
        visible for intermittent short glow spurts
of their long trajectories. Disappear at last, but halfway
        to ghost-dim
        targets. This the longest moment of silence, moment
        of timeless Time. . . .

II.

The longest moment
   is transcribed in the Chief Cannoneer's
journal entry, a cracked page
     of yellow-rimmed parchment framed and bolted
     to the columnar wall of rock
behind the cannon-row
   precipice. A second larger frame
displays a pencil drawing
(details shaded as in a rotogravure news-
     paper photo)—the charred and gutted carcass
       of the Premiere
     Galleon of Napoleon's fleet,

     driven homeward
   in tatters by the "hot shot" surprise
ambush of Nassau's gunners.
     Today, the cannonry master's log notes
     draws us into the harbor mouth
affray. *Seventeen-
Ninety-Three.* Ariel spirits
he'd make of us: a magic
cadence of pure journalism—terror and awe
     in equal shares! We alight on the topmost sails
       of the mainmast,
         his words inflated with the wind

       of bellying canvas,
   puffed sails drawn nearer, nearer. He adjusts
the many interlocked
     segments of the primitive telescope.
     The enchanted eyepiece moves
in and out of focus—
   what a glory of luminous sails
in full blossom! His heart
leaps at the beauty of row upon moonlit row:
     the sails are wings, countless sizes and shapes,

ghostly and fleshlike
in their velvety flutter, so many

wings large and small,
layers and layers mounted to the ladder-
rung multiple tiers
of the tall masts. The ships are sea dragons
flying over the gleamy surface,
so buoyant they appear
to launch airborne leaps, to hover
over the bucking swells,
hung aloft for prolonged moments; all contained,
today, in documentary words of one lordly breath—
the longest moment—
suspended. . . . The cannonballs paled,

flashed and paled, died,
vanished halfway to hellfire. So ravished was he
by the regatta-race
beauty of the fleet of ships, he forgot war,
attackers, his island homeland
under siege. . . *the pirate-*
style pounce of swordsmen, shortrange
musketry firepower
of those teams on shipboard, invincible land
forces if the ships struck shore intact—the bands
of invaders would swarm
like hordes of locusts into the Capitol,

dismantling the seat
of government in so few minutes, all public
buildings incinerated
with torches, the soldiers' barracks firebombed,
unchecked flames blooming into a sea
of fire. . . This fantasy
turns awe to terror—the warrior
in him awakens to a fire
montage, a mental picture swept outward! In two
ships, the highest sails explode—at once—in blood,

    a burst and spatter
    of angry red tongues licking from silk-

   flow layer to layer,
  mast-pole to pole, ropes and cables sizzling
like straw or hay, the white sails
  showing a spark, a tiny speck of scarlet
  at corner or edge, the trickles
hemorrhaging to all ship
  outposts in seconds. A second round
of ammo balls are fired,
a deep tear in mid-hull, bow section split across—
  the crack spreads and spreads. *Heartshot! Those balls*
   of fire, metal
fire carriers, firestorms asleep

   in hurled round missiles.
Napoleon's land militia in Asia—no plains
too wide for their tramp, pillage.
  But fire blooms in the sky at sea, fireballs
  igniting at the top of tallest
masts (matchstick center poles)
  and flamethrower winds puffing downwards—
no stopping them, *no defense*
against the hot ball lightning! Fire brigade dozens
  are climbing the yardarms, rope ladders, swung vines
   of chains. They ferry
  water buckets, wrestling the hoses

   above, yanking water pumps
  below—still spraying faint streams on the maelstrom
of swirling fire, unbroken
  toothless mouth of devouring flame. Their shirts'
  flouncy silk collars and pleated
puff-sleeves catch sparks,
  roasting their necks and exposed backs;
still working the buckets, they slide
down the few intact ropes and chains for refills,
  their body-hair scorched off, their lungs gorged

      with smoke and fine ash. . . .
        Still we linger over the eye witness

            reportage, a lyric
   and breathless stenography of the chief gunner
condensing in two short
   journal entries the mystic timeless moment
   of cannonball flight and soaring.
His life changed twice
   in a gasped breath! Three minutes of sea-
board conflagration scarred
the face of a Titan Colonialist, and sent his few
     surviving ensigns—cast adrift on floating debris,
        scooped up on rafts
        and rescue boats—back to the Continent. . . .

THE DUNGEON AMORIST

(Fort Charlotte, Nassau, Bahamas)

WE IDLE, circling the wide hilltop courtyard of Fort Charlotte,
and bypass the central
square guardhouse—boxlike—which displays
a few stuffed scarecrow
model prisoners, immortally stooped & visible
behind the window bars.
The pebbly surface of our stroll is a roof to the Fort's
labyrinth of underground passageways,
the stone hill's
interior carved by thousands
of slaves

chopping and hacking burrows in rock with the metal pickaxes:
in three years of back-warping
excavations, those chaingangs hollowed out
a hideaway fort
of the interior.... We lift a central trapdoor,
begin our slow descent
into the buried fortress: the upper chambers, mess hall
and living quarters; below, the dungeon
and torture
compartments—long low crawl space,
the upright

narrow cubicles scooped into the floor, each a small arsenal
of ghastly penal hardware
outlasting the victims and mutilators,
alike, for hundreds
of years.... The floors are lit by low portable lanterns,
tucked in random corners.
In each descending staircase, both walls are perforated
by long grooves of varying widths—often,
blasts of air
seem to emit from these apertures

(wind vents,
or ducts?), as if air conditioning pumps had been installed
to cool modern visitors.
But our burly gruff "Bahamahost"
protests—his deep bass,
throaty bulletins delivered with afflatus of blurted
sermons: "Whoosh! Wind flies
through the fort, from hill summit to foot. Wholesome currents
circulate through air flues. No fans, no hidden
A C Units
whirring silently behind the walls—
it's all

natural ventilation. . . ." He bids us reflect upon the genius
of architects who monitored
the mass dig: endless chains of pickax crews,
daily scoopouts of rock
shavings raised from below in canvas sacks, or leather
slings suspended by thick ropes
from pulleys, and carted away in wheelbarrows. They lacked
any supply of low-grade explosives
to shorten
the work time. Reduce the manpower
hours. *Years!*

But excavators of modern mines, despite nitro powder charges,
pile drivers and power drills,
have lost the ultrasonic Ears of those dig
architects—who could hear
deepearth rumbles, the quietest shifts along fault lines.
They sensed the minimal heave
and sway of shelves of quartz and shale miles under the cliff,
miles under the surrounding Carib Sea;
and they guessed
the stablest circuit of tunnels, guessed
the ideal

pattern of flues to conduct the maximum flow of trade winds
through the Fort corridors
and passages. The hums, tones, hisses

and echoes of breezes—
swirling through the magic wind tunnels above—are soughs
of gale winds magnified
in the upper channels. Gull screech and high-pitched wind wails
dissemble inhalation through a giant hurt lung's
bronchial tubes.
The hill of rock draws a breath of its own.
It whirls

around us, ruffling our blouses and shirt sleeves. Currents lick
our ankles. They crawl up
our pant legs, tickle our groins and arm pits.
"Fresh air. Freshened breath.
It is all natural, brother. The natural trade winds cool
man-dug cave passages
of the Fort, natural currents endlessly circulating.
She is my dark Beauty. Oh listen
to her breathing!
She whistles me into her hollows,
lovely wind

channels, her lantern-lit low halls. Now she sweeps me along
on her sighs, wind-wails
of her breath, I, her twenty years inmate
and intimate. She
my gallows, my treasure! Fort Charlotte, my sweet—my secret
delight. . . ." Is it all an act,
a grand Vaudeville charade? Or is he a man in High Love,
demon possessed, the perennial guide
and wanderer
through Fort Charlotte's recesses,
tunnels,

his daily haunts the aisles of her catacomb. . . ? It's a ghoulish
love, a passion for corpses,
we hear chanted in his great barrel-chested
guffaws. *Cadaver love!*
And indeed, her lower chambers are vaults of a tomb: the fort
deeps, fort bottom levels,
are hived with cells of a Folk Mausoleum. The folk myths

                of his robust oratory clamor
                    about the walls!
                He bellows the ill fortunes
                    of hundreds

of limbs torn asunder on stretching blocks, tongues pulled out,
            eyes stabbed with hot pokers:
        the many subtle and varied ingenuities
                of torture mimic—
    grimly—acts of love in his lavish and prolonged lingering
            over details of the horror!
He burbles and snorts a ghastly tableau: layers and layers
        of incinerated bodies, great metal trunks
                of heaped-up ash
            dumped in the sea, at intervals—
                    all drowned

in gushed titters, baritone blasts of hurly-burly laughter!
            And oh, how he loves to hear
        the echoes of his own chortled vibrato
                ricochet from passage
    to passage (*ho-ho-ho*), redoubling through the many cells
            of the honeycomb death house.
This two-hundred-pound bear in his sixties, gray sideburns,
        silver-tinted black beard, for all his loquacious
                spiel billowing
            through the many tunnels of castle
                    underground

as prodigal as the endless bounty of trade winds that pour
            through vent holes—he is tireless!
        His huffing and puffing on stairways is surplus—
                not loss—of breath,
    breath undiminished for all his gargled Falstaffian
            great Belly Laughs. The saga
    of tortured spirits interred in the Fort's Memory Ear
        is soothed, its pain lessened, himself a princely
            host, gentle helpmate
        to the flocks of visitors. He proffers
                    recipes

stylishly worded, for our comfort and safety: a verbal kin
  to actual cane, brace, crutch,
 medicine tablets—his instant and steadfast
  hand under the elbow
of any Soul taking a stair too short, or too fast; shields
  a forehead from batter by low-
hanging rock partition with his dear wide palm (no time
  to howl "Duck!"); spots a trip in a floor crack
   a full half step
  before imperiled footfall; detects
   half-formed

tears in an eye; listens for the half-uttered sobs in a throat
  choked up; whiffs an onset
 of fainting spell before the beleaguered
  face pales and forehead
begins to droop—in time to dispense anodyne of schnapps
  or smelling salts; and dispels
any heartsick pall in the spirit with his heady, roguish,
  slapdash, lumbering jest. . . . As, Mother,
   he feeling—oh!—
  a special endearment to *you,* he bows
   to curtsy

your elf-slight diminutive carriage on each of a dozen-odd
  overlong deep stairs, the steepest
 ramp dropping through a rounded well in the rock,
  last juncture from the Fort
dungeon arena's complex of cells to the hill foot exit,
  a sort of bottom trapdoor.
He promenades you, his slim queenly guest of seventy-five,
  failing to show *no* favoritism to a fellow
   rare Sister
  spirit. You trade movie mag and *National
   Enquirer*

gossip column tales and squibs: the decline of past five U. S.
  Presidents; the rising star
 of Black Women in Bahamian politics
  and world business;

the inside dope on bush-league Bahamian ball players
and middleweight boxers
who are sure bets for world champ futures; the canonization
and crowning of Aretha, the top Soul
or Gospel voice,
today, tomorrow, and beyond the future's
future. . . .

III. Barbados

WOMAN'S TONGUE

Our first daylight drive to Bridgetown... The stream
of traffic, congested
on the narrow
cobblestone roadway, is endless—
but few other cars. It's all foot traffic:
schoolchildren, uniformed, in clusters or smaller
fleets, rarely a single child
walking alone; housewives waddling to and from market,
deep baskets (empty
or full) balanced on their heads;
flocks of goats,
chickens and woolless sheep.... After miles and miles
of tall cane rows, blocking most views of nearby scenery,

shock of blank farmlands, just planted with yams,
beans, vegetable seeds:
we see dozens
of small long-necked white birds,
scattered everywhere, hopping and poking
in the newly-turned soil: cattle egrets (you call them
cowbirds), they're ferreting for lumps,
rich nodules of predigested oats in the fresh manure.
They persevere,
snaring morsels from the dung
droppings, choice
tidbits speared with each peck, each scalpel incision
of those long tapered bills. "Will they deplete all soil

nutrients?" I ask. "What will fertilize the crops?"
"Ha! They rid young sprouts
of killer plant
aphids and pests, a *friend* to crops.
There's enough turds for all, and plenty
to spare." But the regal prancers, springing from dung
cakes to flattened pies, never tire,
never sate their appetites, nip and spear, stab and gorge
their slim bills.

"They should be as obese
as pelicans,"
I say. "How do they stay so slender?" But you brood
upon the avidities of *woman*: open wounds of your divorce—

haunted, still, by images of all love's rewards
and bonuses gone sour.
Grave emblem
sears, flickers before your eyes:
That woman's skull, years after death,
wagging its jawbone up and down, full sets of teeth
chattering yet. The silent jaw—
like an obsolete oil derrick still pumping the drained
well—is cursed
by a nervous tic that defies
rigor mortis.
It keeps jerking open and closed, from side to side,
for eternity, a carryover of the ceaseless nag, bicker,

nitpicking over every trifle, slip—that poisoned
the last years of a twenty
year wedlock.
I shudder! The looming mirage
you grimly lyricize flickers on our wind-
shield (shadows cast by frond tips of the tallest cane);
and worse, I seem to hear skull bones
yammering in the wind. "What is that ghostly crackle
overhead?" I yelp.
Your face a sinister grin, you brake
to a roadside halt,
stepping from the driver's seat and pointing upwards:
"*Woman's Tongue!* See how they flap and creak in the wind!

So many Woman Tongues in motion at once." I stretch
my neck through the car window,
while taking in—
at a glance—whole galaxies
of the flat tongueshaped dried pods, dangled
from the tops and all visible fringes of the long row
of trees bordering the road edge.

When the wind blows, they all shake and rattle in chorus.
I could mistake them
for a vast flock of black grackles
or warblers,
but for your verbal notation: "Hear them whisper
and hiss—like women *shushing*," you say. Your eyes roll,

as if they put you in a trance, and when the wind
grows stronger, the shush sounds—
oddly isolate
and distinct in light breezes—
become a single irreducible crackle,
which spreads and spreads in the distance around us. . .
And you say, "That's the way it was
when the whirlwind of marriage blew hardest, that army
of vile locusts
sizzling and roaring. Behind
any casual hurt
or misgiving, the din became impossible to escape,
the whole world of sound given over to the drawn-out

flapping of those unstoppable tongues." *Wind dies.*
Grating clatter upon our ears,
moments before,
lulls to a stammer, the few clicks
spaced out—at intervals—from one end
of the thick clump of trees to the other. *Soft rattlings.*
Those quiet aftershocks, residues
of pandemonium of vengeful tongue-clucks, tongue-sputters,
seem more noiseless
than silence itself. And in this sad
epilogue, knell
to our fierce chorale of furies, you recall tender
passing laments of early betrothal—pain quickly dulled,

the mournful voice but one quaver from gay teasing;
those easier griefs shaken
by a straw's tickle
under the chin, your wife's tongue
flirting with the bass notes of the dirge.

Her voice softened with kisses and laughter, she'd relent
to the gentle wind's caress,
as do these immature pods in late fall and winter, rinds
still moist and green.
But in the long hot season, their skins
grow thin and taut—
they dry out quickly! The pods wilt, a one-year cycle.
There's no turning back. The trees lose their leaves in May

and June, exposing the dried pods to roughest winds
in the season of storms—
toward the day
of the last worst gusts. *Midsummer.*
All the Woman Tongues fibrillate at once,
like heart muscles run amok—they wildly tremble and quake,
taking small comfort from matched
agonies of their fellow tongue flutterers, their comrades
in dry-voiced angers;
the dried-out pods, cracked and flaking,
fall to earth. . . .
New whole forests of Woman's Tongue trees, it is said,
may spring from a single burst-pod's wind-wafted seedlings.

THE TELEPHONE PIRACIES

1.

LAST NIGHT, you soaked the chicken parts in a thick lime marinade,
        the chunky breasts, backs
    and thighs submerged wholly in the deep ceramic dish. You thin-sliced
        dozens of small eggplants—
blackish-purple blunt snouts leaking droplets, still, from gaps
      where you yanked them from young vines—and you simmered the chips
        on the hot plate, fresh
    and lightly cooked for today's beach sunrise picnic....
      I waken

to steady trickling of water below my bed, three loud spurts followed
        by gurgled swift currents
    streaming under the floorboards. I leap to the window, my eyes half-
        stuck with sleep mucilage,
to check out my mental tableau of floodwaters risen,
      and tugging at the baseboards of this country house: I see
        the roof pitched sideways
        as the house—ripped from its four corners—careens
        like a ship

sinking, its planks of cedar siding split apart; the whole edifice,
        uptorn, is dragged,
    collapsing, across the furrowed pasturage of Barbados' rolling hills
        to sea.... I settle myself
at the window: the pounding on the wall your hammer
      nailing a few hoops of cyclone fencing to the front door post;
        the gush of water
        a fierce outpouring from two wide-mouthed hoses, spigots
        twisted

to the limit, those two streams rapidly drenching the acres of fruit
        and vegetable gardens
    you hastily installed these past few months, which totally encircle
        the wood frame ranch house. Your home
    appears to be marooned in a sea of leafs, stems, vines

and veggies, tall bean stalks sending tendrils and mature beans
    upwards into the eaves,
  the drain pipes—melons knocking on the window sills.
    They creep

visibly higher as I watch! Squash and eggplant shapes are tumbled
    into the little walkways
  between plant rows like tame wildlife (gophers, rabbits, raccoons?)...
    This will be the honeymoon chateau—
  you rhapsodize—for your betrothed, happy switchboard
    operator, two seas and one continent distant in Chicago's
      Loop: six months blossomed
    toward your baby's arrival day, she tending your other
      lush garden....

2.

   That buzzing! Repeats
  and repeats, behind us: it has continued—
without letup—for five minutes,
  I recall, absently. *A telephone ring.*
  Unfamiliar chimes, to my ear.
"Yes," you smile. "Starts
  at 5 A.M. sharp, daily. Persists.
Gets louder and funnier.
Until I hear the bells shriek over hoses'
  glug-glug, clicks of my pruning, clomp of boot
   cleats; and, today,
  as you see, it even outsquawks

   drone of our chatter."
So saying, your happy lilted hum resumes.
You take slow steps across the porch,
  shake mud from shoes, slip off boots, and tromp,
  barefoot, over kitchen linoleum
to the phone receiver.
  The next moment, I'm answering "Hello"
to a voice at the nerve center
of ten thousand wires and electro-magnetic
  coils wound in a transatlantic gasket, larynx
   of Chicago switchboard:
   she, your affianced, who controls

   fragile speech hook-ups
  between multitudes of tongues in all seven
continents by the magic plugs
  she fits into thin sockets on the sparking peg
  boards. Happy groans from St. Louis
crisscross rebel grunts
  and threats from Guyana, interlaced
with mystic wails of half-starved
Haitian refugees phoning *collect* from Key West
  public waystation booths to their foster parents,
   or parole officers
   in Port-au-Prince.... Other voices,

    other sighs, are always
  cutting in, skirting tail ends of our blurted
dialogue. "But wait!" she says,
  "Hang up, a moment. I'll phone back, and try
  for a better connection." And I,
bedazzled, picture her
  necromancing the many straw-hole-sized,
gaping mouths of that vast peg map,
erasing the snippets and tagends of ghostly
  intruder voices, throats trying to come back
   from other worlds,
    other ages—past and future:

  from death. . . Ah, she knows
  she has the lordly power to cleanse the wires
with quick shifts of her plugs,
  or buttons pushed on her portable computer.
  She waves off all interference,
scrubs out static, chirr,
  hum or buzz from the private hot line
between us (most underseas
cables subject to her immediate wish,
  or command). Phone rings crisper, her renewed
   voice so acutely clear,
   she looms close; your tall man-

    shape fades far. You pace
  from side to side as we, your sweetheart and I,
warble the tunes of first meeting.
  She muses upon her plans for her new life,
  her baby's, and next she elicits
my glanced pre-view
  of her future Island home. I translate
quick eye sketch of house layout,
garden, farms nearby, into verbal jottings—
  nourish happy fancies of her baby's nursery
   and stomping grounds.
    "Tell Bruce, the baby just kicked,

turned, it hears my thoughts—
it listens, yes, eavesdrops on all that we say,
prenatal ears the perfect
    bugging device. *They miss nothing.* Whatever
    words pass between us, across
the wires, the baby hears
    and stores up, for our future Carib-
bean life. If you come visit
our home, Larry, he'll know you from the Other
    world. Speak, again! I hold the phone's earpiece
        to my abdomen.
    He'll remember your voice, ever. . . ."

    And I, too, a believer
in the phone wire's ultrasensory powers,
I dream the coaxial cable's
    genius to squeeze the millions of human voices
    into a six-inch-thick wave pulse
conductor. . . I dream, again,
    the waking dream of wires twisting
and looping between our ears,
piercing rocky cliffs, scaling mountain heights,
    traversing both sea floors and her unborn child's
        veins and arteries,
        its neurons and unfinished nerve

    endings, the small bones
and slowly developing softer cartilages
of the foetus's middle ears.
    She, like a snake charmer, performs the rites
    with snaps of her wrist. Snake heads
of the plugs, burying
    their silvered fangs, flash and flash
in her magnetic peg board!
Wires pinching her wrists are charm bracelets,
    the earphone wires around her neck, a sorceress's
        necklace—her arms
        and neck vibrate those circuit

        whips with her own thrilled
    nerve fire! That energy surges from her voice
to my capillary receptors,
    and I tingle. My skin prickles. I hear
    with my very pores her globe-
spanning electric pulse
    that flows through serpents of wires,
cables, her child's thin pipes
and half-formed spinal branchings. . . She twines
    all pickups in the unborn, the justborn, the twice
      born: the baby,
        myself, her divorced husband-to-be. . . .

3.

        This universe
     is one closed-circuit Home Box
    Office switchboard, and she, the skilled
  architect of *better connections*. With the secret zeal
    of CB truck radio buffs
 flashing signals to their fellow truckers in the rear,
  warning them to keep
a watch for traffic control troopers,
  "smokies," parked

       behind the bill-
     boards, teamed up with radar
    helicopters overhead (true grit tough
  opponents)—she offers to splice an illegal circuit,
    a triangular phone hitchup
  between Miami Beach and Barbados by way of Chicago! It's
 a crime of airwave
electronics piracy, a felony
  of sorts, she

      a folk outlaw
    of the overseas family
    world comedy—woman Robin Hood
  of the global wire forest, wedding my Carib voice
    to my mother's far Florida
    voice. . . "A crisis *Act of Mercy*," she says, "if unlawful
  into the bargain,
but I'm quitting my switchboard
  supervisor's job

      in two months,
    anyhow, the better to relish
    my last seven weeks of pregnancy
  prior to *exile*—my emigration to Barbados, for life. . ."
    While I'm pondering the ethics
    of her pledge to hot wire an instant mother-son liaison,
  she ignores my lapse,
and inserts her nimble plugs: *I*
follow a just

    impulse, she says,
   prompted by *your terror, Larry*—
  upon hearing the grave news of Liberty
 City Race Riots, begun at the very hour of my flight
  from Miami, eight days ago.
My week-long isolation from all news media in the flux
 and whirligig
of Island-hopping. And today,
 my panic!

   Fear for mother's
  safety, her apartment highrise
  thick in the vortex of that crime war
 flare-up. . . . *Now mother's happy shouts, mine, relayed*
  through an eight-word deadpan tone
  declaring station-to-station overseas caller to called.
 Disbelief. Safety,
on both sides, assured. We, by our guardian
 outlaw, joined. . . .

CANE FIRES

Most plantation slaves,
freed in eighteen-thirty-four, stayed on,
tenant sharecroppers tilling the same plots, one hundred squares miles
of cane acreage, over half of Barbados'
land area—cane rows stretching as far
as we can see, in all directions. . . . Today, the Island's
misshapen avocado layout is so clogged
with cane, all visitors must drive
to outlying shores for unobstructed views. *I can believe a total*
usurpation of land by sugar cane, the vast
amoeba's sprawled pseudo-

podia engulfing all square
tracts of tillable earth, the population
of farmer sugar sheiks camped out on straw pallet beds in furrows—
aisles between cane rows: they'd live
on a diet of pure cane juice and sugar
byproducts, no space left for vegetable crops or homes. . . .
We stop at the country stand vender's
cart: fresh-cut whole stalks of cane
are fed into the mouth and tubular throat (ostrich gullet?) of a machine
that grinds tough cane poles into stringy
pulp, pure cane nectar

poured into our held-out
cups (Carib kin to Florida orangecrusher
apparatus), and we drink—not a *sweetened* beverage—but pure extract
of sweetener itself. The tang, tincture
of sour or tart, is akin to suckled
morning glory stems. Or wine of just-picked dandelion
roots. We are floating back in Nature's
juice cycle to "unimproved" elixirs
that nourish the plants' threading vesicles directly. . . We resume our cross-
country tour, passing cane fields in all stages
of cutting and harvest:

crops full-grown, we find
more and more fields picked clean, or levelled,

oddly, to ash and burnt-edge stumps of fronds, charred roots. Some plants,
        still smoking, cough sparks, fallen cane
        embers aglow from fires in progress,
    if nearly extinguished. Perhaps one in three, of those fields
        harvested, reveals scars, limbs scorched
        or shrivelled, while entire quadrants
of cane acres are blackened (a corner here, front rows there); or whole farms
        appear burnt to the ground, plants devoured
        by the flames as midsummer

        firestorms scavenge forests. . . .
The work of arsonists, I wonder? And yet,
the cane fires are so widespread, how could a few outlaws, warring against
        the many planters, remain at large?
        Half the Island would be up in arms—
    thousands of farmhands, joining the sheriff's posse, scour
        all hideaway nooks and remote caves
        in the hills, hunting the fugitives.
I fancy the poor fire-crazy runaways smoked out of hiding by strategic
        brushfires, or bayed up trees by police-trained
        wolf hounds, raw leg shank

        or ankle frozen, perhaps,
        in bear-trap's sawtoothed bite. . . . We pass
an overlarge cane field, a single plantation extending beyond the limits
        of sight on the long stretch of road
        before us, sprawling on both sides
    of our thread of blacktop, negligible subdivider. I'm struck
        by the paced teamwork of a dozen, or more,
        young men running with torches aflame,
each touching his firebrand to dry sticks of cane, brownish fronds, skilled
        at finding every plant's most flammable
        patch, or vulnerable edge—

        spots chosen flaring up,
    yellow flames deepening to purply red
in the core of larger plants, windswept into a blaze. . . . Now a second troop
        of fieldhands follows close upon heels
        of the torch bearers (these the fire-

fighters?), carrying sheets, rags, old blankets: they spread
    wide their cloaks of linen or canvas
       over hottest fires, choking the flames
and blanketing the acrid-smelling smoke fumes, thin trails of sugar serum
    bubbly and sizzling, wheresoever flame-ups
       are smothered. Half-oxidized

       sugar aroma, the foetor
    of pig lard rendered over open gas flames
(that, too, spitting and gurgling!), burns our eyes, nostrils. *Ammoniac.*
    But seductive. Roast suckling pig, buried
       in a shallow pit, emits like fragrance
during the last half-hour of browning and crackling on a bed
    of white-hot coals. The odors attract
       and repel, at once; saliva rush oscillates
with mild nausea. I keep wanting to savor the burning granules—to taste,
    but not to inhale, the heavy organic smoke
       stench. *Asphyxiating....*

       The departed torch crew
    returns, swinging machetes. They split and hack
seared lengths of cane, those flame-singed snapping off at machete flicks;
    others having to be struck, again and again—
       as axes chop logs: all severed poles
and rods of cane abandoned, helter-skelter, where they fall
    (lengths varied from six feet to two-foot
       stovepipe stumps charred at one end),
no interrupting this samurai sabre dance of men wielding machetes, to gather
    their harvest. Soon they're followed by a return
       of the backup team, men

       grasping tarps, serapes,
    shawls, which they convert to arm-hoists. Backpacks.
Each worker collects a thick bundle of scattered sugar tubes, tying a cord
    around the pile and dragging his burden
       across the field's furrow troughs;
    or hauling the load on his shoulder, balanced in the homemade
       cloth sling... "What's the point of ritual
       fire games?" I ask. "The Canepickers' Union

have devised ways to speed up our labor," you reply, "since the men are paid
       by the job—so many cane tons cut and hauled—
          not by the hour, or workday;

          and thus, elaborate rites
       of torching the cane, care taken to stifle
fires before they roast through to the sugar cores. This action, you see,
       stiffens the cane rinds. Many can be cut
         quickly, perhaps three per swing of machete—
   which triples the work pace, work capacity. But the fires,
       even *short* burns, kill guardian fruit flies
        which feed on cane pests, most flies wiped out,
alas, before they lay thousands of eggs and breed new offspring, a progeny
       to police next year's cane glut." "But how,"
         I ask, "do you explain *this*

         cane field, like two others
      we passed today, every square foot of land
covered with plant ash, or smoking cinders; a few root stubs or stumps afire,
       still, from the recent incinerations?" . . .
       The sport of felons, you admit (*terrorists,*
    or the like): *they play a prank on the farmers, starting fires*
      at night—dousing plants with kerosene, then
      lighting a long fuse to the single firebomb:
swift inferno and holocaust of the whole field—assassin nowhere to be seen,
       when a fire typhoon whirls itself into one
         quenchless wave of flame!

FAIRCHILD MARKET: MEATS AND MAUBY

(Bridgetown, Barbados, 1981)

MIDDAY SUN, between two big cloud-
   bursts: the heat and press of shoppers closer,
      more sweltering, for steam and mists arisen from standing pools
         in the maze
            of streets enveloping the vast sweep
of open market... Most of the outdoors merchants and venders—
      during downpours—
   hurriedly cover their stocks and produce

with old newspapers, or thin plastic
   liners, and take refuge themselves under roof
      overhangs of the central indoors shopping mall. *As do I.*
         Sheltered space,
            in the mile long market interior,
seems to expand without limit, to left and right, but I head
      straight for the glass
   faced tall vertical display cases in the rear.

Two immense ox carcasses, dangled
   from wall hooks, signify the meat department.
      I read the plaque, given prominent highlighting on the wall
         above two gnarled
            chopping blocks, juxtaposed on the blood-
   and-entrail-smeared counter: KEEP IT CLEAN   YOUR MIND
      YOUR BODY   THE WORDS OF YOUR MOUTH
   THIS MARKET   BARBADOS   CLEANLINESS IS

NEXT TO GODLINESS   Butchers
   scurry to and fro, a few taking rest breaks
      from hauling and dressing sides of beef, lamb & goat, to chat
         with customers,
            old friends. A dozen or more butchers'
stalls, side by side, are separated by low pasteboard partitions.
      So rarely idle,
   they squeeze all sales, packaging and transactions

between swings at the blocks. One jumbo
>meat cleaver, as long as a machete, quivers,
>>its full length stuck upright in the block, vibrating like a knife-
>>>thrower's flung blade—
>>>>no time for the cleavers to grow still
>>between beefsides. The armory of knives—whether swung at meat hunks
>>>or trembling in blocks—
>>>seems to direct the whole slaughter scenario:

relay teams of meat carriers,
>heavy sluggers on the chopping decks, and refined
>>trimmers of the more elegant cuts of meat. The whistling cleavers,
>>>razor sharp slicers
>>>>lopping off waste scraps of gristle and fat—
>>a whole family of knives, ranging from penknifesized paring tools
>>>to small hatchets
>>>and axes: this widely diverse repertoire

of bludgeons, cutters and choppers:
>this host of implements—luxuriantly stained
>>and clotted and polished—grace and adorn the rough-hewn segments
>>>of debarked stumps.
>>>>*Do the freshly sawed tree slabs impart*
>>*a unique savor, or tang, to the carcasses dismembered and carved*
>>>*thereupon? To knives? . . .*
>>Now three chief butchers, in adjacent stalls,

commence whopping full sides of beef
>at once—are they an accidental ensemble? Or do
>>the two on either side take cues for rhythm and hacking stroke
>>>from the middle man?
>>>>A large audience gathers, who admire
>>the performance, however many times they've seen it before. A few
>>>young spectators,
>>>in their mid-twenties, perhaps, are primped up

with gold chains, necklaces; their costumes
>aflame with bright colors, bands and twists of silk.
>>I presume they are a local cult group who visit the meat market,

daily, to applaud
    feats of the knife-wielding maestros. . . .
Though I stand back a few steps, an exile from the occult inner
    circle of viewers, I
stand *out,* more the intruder for trying to hide,

to be invisible. The middlemost
   butcher quits in mid-swing, interrupts a moment
      of high passion in the swift honing of loin edges, the severance
         of key shoulder joints,
            hip joints, to ask after my scratchy pen
   markings. I pretend (with all eyes present now upon me) to sketch
      a freehand drawing,
      but no one is fooled: my scrawled words of journal

entries, observed by many before,
   give me away: "Ya wan sum meat, bruda, or ya
      jus doin reee-surch?" And before I can display a grimly hurried
         fake line drawing
            of the ox leg-shank, he has resumed
   the knife-juggling art, while humming the notes for current pop
      hit calypso songs
      and exchanging choice scraps of local gossip

and scandal. Some three or four separate
   crisscrossing trajectories of talk may flourish
      at once, all seemingly led by this one interlocutor, as gifted
         a spiel maker
            as meat caterer and decorator,
   his mixed media gabble all rolled into the one meat-slaughterhouse
      argot. . .   C. W. CARTER
      MEAT DEPOT: thick black script, a calligrapher's

art, painted on the red aprons—two ties
   around neck and waist—worn by the head meat hackers
      who, in the final stages of dressing family sized roasts, chops
         and soup bones, grow
            careless, and let fly fragments, bone chips

zinging one way, wood slivers and flakes another, pointing the wisdom
   of thick rubber goggles
  worn by the eldest meat veteran (would they had

spare pairs of the specs for standers-by);
  those watching from front row close-ups cup their hands
    over their brows: they could be blinded! "Watchasuf dehr, fella," I
     dodge to one side
       of his sprinter's beeline, just in time.
 How can he trot so fast on his heels, red-becapped and black-rubber-
    coated, the slick coat tails
  flopping about his bare sockless ankles, feet

in sneakers (soaked in a mixture of ox
  blood, drool, and soapy water), hugging to his chest
    two whole sides of slaughtered livestock, one goat, one sheep: mutton
     towering a foot,
       or more, over his head. As he runs,
 a duck's side-to-side waddle, he bonks the low-hung wood frame timbers
    and an exposed light bulb
    dangled from a thirty-foot-long wire attached

to the roof. He struggles with his hugged
  cargos, flashing a queer smile—*he might be a man*
    who daydreams he embraces two lovers of different Races. He's
     a Romeo, I'm told,
       by a co-worker. And quite a classy
    dresser. *All of his three-piece suits are double-breasted. . . .* Everyone
     cheers the arrival,
    through the rear doorway (which I now see leads

to the canopy-low-roofed fish market):
  a shrivelled twinkly eyed woman in her nineties,
    Mag, a great favorite of the group. All ages rejoice in the salute!
     She drags a low
       push cart, a tall steamy cauldron
 on the top shelf. The spigot cock attached to the base regulates
    the flow of the barrel's
    liquid contents through a rubber tube below.

In moments, she has filled dozens of paper
 cups for most nearby shoppers. Still others race
  to our checkpoint from all aisles of the market's labyrinth,
   when Mag shakes her hand
    bells, and squeaks in a barely audible
voice, "Mauby, Mauby!" Now two of the master butchers deliver
  sacks of wood bark, lugged
   from their stalls' rear corners: mostly odd shapes,

whole circular chunks or crowbar-pried scraps,
 the bulk removed intact from their freshly debarked
  chopping blocks. They deposit the contents of the bags in broad
   cartons on her wagon's
    lower shelf; she to take home the bark hoops,
 bark shingles, and boil them, so to perfect her own secret brew
  of thick syrupy Mauby,
   the Bajans' native stock of Coca Cola. . . .

BARBADOS DROUGHT SONGS

I. Menopause of the Cowherds

*Vivid flux of light shifts   Ghost lights of Barbados
daybreak*. . . . My first shimmery views
  of the land since last night's short airport
    commute. Mists, slowly rising from coast pastures,
      are marked, here and there,
        by horizontal low lines.
          I follow the streaks of brown, tracing their course
            to shadow-puffs afloat
        at either end. *Dark boulder shapes
      near the shoreline   Narrow columns
    of smoke inland, trailing behind.* . . . Oh, it's a lonely
  stop-and-go trailblazer
operation that I, blearily, oversee,
  searching in haze for telltale flash of mottled
    hide; or for poised human hand,
      palmside turned skyward, the rope-
        end twined around its appended wrist: both clues
          to the drugged identities
      of creatures joined by the rope lengths.
    Man and cow. The latter leads
      her indolent master in slow perambulations, now
  moving in wide circles,
now shifting course—she tugs a zigzag path
  to shore. . . . In five or ten minutes, the fog bank
    has lifted: I can make out
      six separate and discrete
        cowherds, draggled this way and that by their nose-
          downward slackjawed charges
        munching hither and thither, but snouts
      unslaked, rooting in dust puffs,
    begging scorched vegetation. The languid farmhands,
  I now discern, carry
long thin rods; they are poking and inspecting
  the earth for patches of wildgrass or sedge, remnants
    of near-depleted pasture.

    At last, two men—in opposite
        corners of my bedroom window vista—begin
            driving wooden stakes
        into cracked topsoil (their choicest
        feeding sites look as bare of flora
    as most of the rejected quadrants). . . . A sudden jump
  in their energy output
suggests goldminers staking claims, yet they slump
  in poses of instant siesta, just outside their cows'
        chomping perimeters.
            How swiftly each famished creature
            gobbles any shred, leaf or root of edible
                wisp within its reach,
            scraping deep into earth for the bulbs
        underground, then flopping down
    at tether's end, following a few heartless yanks
    at restraining stakes. Wild fodder,
plentiful in other years, created this habit
  of search and stop and chaw and root in the earth—
        a reflex anachronism!
            Cow and man, both locked in a nerve
                rote impulse: so strong an antique faith
                    in returns from *Earth*
                Mother, they'd scratch at dead tree
            stumps, bare rock, gaping ruins
        of sandstone quarry, archaeological excavation
    sites—and still believe, ever,
  in regrowth of the tip of bud, shoot, leaf,
    or root. That bovine creed (a healing art, perhaps)
        could *will* fresh roots
            from the dead stump, or prime live
                shoots from withered stalks. But these cowherds,
                    cows, dally and droop, side-
                by-side, the long day's sluggish withdrawal
            from quest already begun. . . .

II. A Frieze of Sheep

Gray fog cover lifts   The ceiling slowly moves
higher, but darker   Black
thundercloud mass
drifts inland from the seacoast. . . .
A line-up of sheep edges
into my window. Some twelve or fourteen adult sheep,
I count off, marching in strict head-
to-tail formation, their cues signalled by voices
in the rear: two
teenagers, a boy and a girl
in tattered patchwork
dungarees, flicking their poles at hindquarters
of a couple of fattest sheep stooped on bent forelegs

to rest, holding up the train. Boy snaps his whip,
a birchen switch. Wobbly,
the large old sheep
jerks forward. A steady pace resumes. . . .
I now see four baby sheep (one
falling on its side or rump, repeatedly), stragglers
trailing the pair of shepherds
by a short distance. Quite near our hilltop yard,
the sheepgirl taps
a halt with her stick's flat edge.
The whole flock
responds, wandering short arcs to left and right,
stooping to chew wisps of root, odd clumps of crabgrass.

The foliage, though scant, affords springy tufts
for each softfaced full-lipped
nibbler. . . Wha! Sand
jumps, appears to be alive, skipping
in the lowered sheep faces,
dust-whirls stirred about the skimpy scrub brush. Oh, look!
It's fat half-dollars and quarters
of rain falling. Thick droplets, splattering, kick up
dry patches of dust.

Next moment, water falls in sheets
of solid rain,
flat planes of wet catching the light reflected
from the inlet bay at different angles, thinnest walls

of water turning, like panels of revolving doors,
facing many directions:
the glassy walls
flash and flash, even as I watch
(never before have I seen
such a demoniac sudden downpour), and what a change
has come over the stunned sheep!
Each one frozen in place, as if turned to stone,
they are immobile
as statues—a couple bent over,
their necks stiff
in the pose of eating, but the faces don't budge
an inch, the jaws unmoving. Others in varied postures:

one young buck with twisted neck and head thrown back,
in hysteric shock, it seems
(a lordly stallion
whinnying its high-pitched shriek,
its threat, before it bolts
or attacks an aggressor, but holding that difficult
upswung position without a flinch
or quaver). Still other sheep are fixed in plaster
moulds, their color,
even, altered from tawny hues
to ashen greys,
stony offwhites. . . . Now both junior caretakers
are agitated, leaping from one stalled four-legged

sculpture to another, prodding with their poles—
to no effect. They chide
their shellshocked
numb livestock, but know it's useless.
They have seen instant deepfreeze
of rain paralysis before (not this drought season,
maybe), but the boy—in fury—

throttles the large buck across the nose. Unbudged.
Not a twitch!
He might be whipping an upright
corpse petrified
in rigor mortis, though the four infant sheep
cavort in the rain like kittens, rolling on their sides

and backs, shattering the instant puddles swelled
by the one-minute cloud burst.
Rain halts. Quits,
utterly, in seconds, as sudden
as it began. No single
drops visibly plopping in the few bright slick spots,
or small pools that formed. The adult
sheep, as if stung by electric cattle prods, spring
out of their coma,
instantaneously. They commence
relaxed feeding,
a few new leaf sprouts turned up by the showers—brief
downpours flirt with plant tops, but shortchange the roots.

IV. St. Lucia

QUEEN OF THE BILLIARDS

On the first eve of Carnival, night of the Queen
  contest, I dine on the hostel
    terrace overlooking Castries' Harbor.
      The hostess, much
        senior to the teenage waitresses,
      mid-twenties, say (svelte
    in lustrous black taffeta dress; short cape
  with lace trim), takes elegant slow steps, escorting me
    to the premiere Harbor View
        two seat table. Then she sidles
          out the back door, nods to the hidden bar hostess, drops off
            her high heels and—in one long stride—scoops
              a pair of slippers with upcurled toes. She shuffles

across a hardwood floor to join a tense parlor game
  in progress in the smoke-filled
    back room, she the absentee participant
      whose next shot
      is so nervously awaited—
    the expectant hush
    draws me to the rear exit. Unobserved,
  poised behind the decorative carved door jamb, I peer
    at a fast-moving game
        of billiards. Three agile men compete
          with the black-gowned hostess, her moves with a cue stick
            swift, exact, wholly free of excess.
          The electric snap of her delicate thin wrists,

her eel-like slender black arms, crisp pop of the cue
  and click of ball upon ball—
    all bespeak a style near flawless. Two men,
      distant friends
      to the proprietary couple
      (manager, chief hostess),
    dressed in knockabout leisure suits,
  tease and snicker, warmly, between her virtuoso
    shots. Her calls, delivered

        in sharp creole patois ("seeks bawl
    in de syd pahk't, Mon"), elicit fond jeers—so relaxed,
       they forgive her for winning. Their eyes
        applaud her talent! But the manager, in *Dreadlocks*

hairdo, three-piece suit and suspenders, who is
  courting her and hates to lose
    (failed wooer, too, I'd hazard), casts zigzag
      finger shadows
       across the aimed trajectory
  of her next slow shot.
  When the chicanery of finger
puppets flops, her lucky streak unchecked, he performs
    hexy hand-hoops, fists and Vs
      over the ball, circling the chalked tip
        of her cue stick in motion (waist-bent, he shakes the broad
        table with his reach), chanting voodoo
      curses and bugaboos. . . She frowns, but tolerates

his worst pranks. They are his *Reggae* prerogative.
  At last, she misses a routine
    flick shot. He snatches the cue from her, lines up
      his ricochet
      side-cushion poke with great flourish:
    Rastafarian who stalks
    prize game, he executes
his combinations with princely attack, palms thumping
    the velvet table top—a drum beat. . .
        He whoops a cry of triumph, two classic Ace
      shots in a row! Then, murderous quiet bathes the gnat-thick
        hall. Individual dust motes divebomb
        the table like a storm of asteroids, meteorites. . . .

Hand slips, in mid-shot. The long tapered rod squirms,
  jiggles in his grip, and the ball
    flies askew. Leaps the hurdle of side cushion. Cracks
      glass panelling
    in the antique double doors. "Scratch,"
  she murmurs, while he,
  in fury, swings the cue back and forth

like a cracked whip, rips the felt cover from end to table
  end, exposing the unfinished
      wood—flesh pink—beneath the gash. "Foul play.
    You jumped!" he threatens her. Now both men restrain his arms,
    while—the cue stick smashed across his knee—
      he waves wood icicle spears, Zululike, with each hand. . . .

DOMINOES AND POLITICS ON THE MORNE

(Morne Fortuné, Castries, St. Lucia)

      Your Downisland Legend
precedes you in my travel Almanac. In Barbados,
tops in your college class—one month before graduation, you quit!
     For three years, a dropout: *ideals*
      must not be compromised. And no one
  could guess what task or ceremony blocked your finish,
      so close to a degree. . . . Apartments
     and bungalows seem honeycombed,
randomly, in all shelves, ledges and overhangs of Morne Fortuné
   (the mountain rising directly behind Castries'
      town square): the odd

      displacement of house
  lots defies zone or subdivision layout, portions
of military quarters exhumed from one hundred years disuse. . . *Midday.*
     Sunny. Blazing glare flashed
      from corrugated zinc or tin rooftops—
blinding me to a halt at every turn of the tangly uphill
    road: tar wet and sticky: a two way
      single lane blacktop which ties
knots or loops in itself so quickly, some higher bends in the road
   seem to undercut, or tunnel below, the curves
      we left behind. "Turn

      here," you say. We drop
  into a burrow—I slam the brakes to a stillstand,
three feet from the road: private drive and car port (one car limit!)
    serving eight or nine homes stacked
      one upon another, slantwise,
  like a ten story cliff pagoda carved into the mountainside,
     the row of vague roof-gutter
      projections the only visible proof
of demarcations between overhead levels. The old military barracks
    and canteen were slid into natural indentations
      in the hillslopes: hide-

               away, camouflage to fool
     enemy ships at sea—just entering the harbor mouth.
But why do modern contractors and architects keep up this buried facade?
            Homes, not military trenches
            or dugouts—"Foxholes!" I think,
  as we step down the ramp into a low basement cottage, all light
            blocked out by heavy shutters. I
            am sightless, for a full minute,
perhaps. Hear the oscillations of rockers beneath a chair in the corner.
      Heavy breathing in tempo with to-and-fro creaks
           of the rocker. Grandfather,

            is it? Or Great-great. . . I'm
    greeted by sodden handshake. *Gnarled damp roots,*
knobby, cold, rotted in spots, dug up fresh from loose soil. But I drop
            the limp claw of putty, and steal
            past the makeshift partition—
  a halfdrawn curtain suspended from the ceiling on a flexible
            wooden rod—into an alcove (the "bahk
            room"), where your young wife nurses
a days-old wrinkled, hairless monkey with human ears. I greet numerous
     other family members, spanning four generations:
           seated; standing on one leg,

           storklike; leaning upon wall,
  or door jamb, I taking no more than two steps
between kin, and we're thrust out the door into blinding sun. My eyes
          still hadn't adjusted to the indoors
          dimmed light, no one face grown
  detailed enough to grasp, or remember. . . . Now we're circling
          higher and higher, en route to *Top*
          of the Morne, above all dwellings—
a panoramic view of nearby islands, then lunch at the famed native Inn,
    public lodge revered for its ethnic cuisine:
          melting pot and nerve

          center, where island
   dignitaries, artists, and common laborers sup
side-by-side, rub shoulders. And even as we pass through the portico
         (men and boys seated at the domino

     tables), you hobnob with a uniformed
  V.I.P., tall and elegant: his open-throated khaki jacket,
     oddly formal, styled after Castro's
      dishabille manner, but sporty—
not militiaman—attire (no stiff cloth bars on the shoulder, or breast
    decorations, but the sinister aroma of gunpowder
      musk is in our breaths)...

      Two-minute convivialities.
   Intros. Poet to Poet to Deputy Prime Minister,
the first word of the lofty title spoken ten decibels softer. Degrees,
     honors, from Oxford and Bristol,
      are sprinkled like condiments
  in the comic salad of our brief doorway repartee—our air
      of breakneck comings and goings,
      feigned laxity, feigned ease. Upright,
we hover, as at attention. Waved good-byes, leaden, flicker between us,
  while we part company. Two seconds out of earshot,
      your voice much subdued,

     "He's to be sworn in—
    advanced to Prime Minister—within a Fortnight!
Were I *your* guest, in Illinois, small chance I'd ever met Veep Mondale
     in a local snackshop, or bistro."
      I nod my assent... The expatriate
  poet, diplomaless, was lauded at his homecoming—a hero's
      welcome. His Island patrimony
      is status: known to a few seated,
not to others, *all* sense a nimbus of starlight, moondust, he inhabits....
    We linger, waiting to be seated by an absentee
      host—happily surrounded

      by seven gaming tables.
    Dominoes! At one end of the screened gallery,
a child of six is locked in a dead heat with a man four generations
      his senior. With each slow move
      of the white-eyed black tablets,
  the barrier of decades, or social strata, between players
      melts away. Skill at the tables
      breeds a high pitch of listening,

which seems to infuse the room's smoke-billowy updrafts with an aura
 of quiet brooding. . . . A slender winged bulb (*a Dali
 ear?*) streaks from table

 to table, pauses *in air*,
 its wings a blue shimmery blur. We know it hears
all the gaming voices, and it sights the white domino-eyes wink news
 of wins, news of losses. It winks
 back, jerks toward the ceiling
 as if yanked upwards by a window-shade spring, then stops
 on a dime of light just below
 the one bare electric bulb—stalls
in place for slow whirred seconds: its purple pate glisters, lustrous
 in the glare. Now it zooms a diagonal descent
 to chair-back four tables

 distant, hovers as if set
 to alight on this empty chair between two fidgety
mustachioed opponents, but zips down to the adjacent chair's lower rung
 between ankles. A two-second landing!
 Next, it drifts under the table
 and emerges betwixt the knees of one who rises from his seat
 in a victory shout. . . Suddenly, I
 notice you're tracing the hummingbird's
last moves for me with your finger, pointing and orchestrating his swerves:
 "Oh, how he thrives on the smoke-filled effluvium
 of the domino tables, swings

 their luck one way today,
 tomorrow the other; so tame, he flies bull's-eyes
through the oldest man's cigar smoke hoops." "Just so, I've seen hummers
 before," I say, "in California. But never
 a family-tamed homing pigeon: Good Luck
 augurer and household pet into the bargain, who sips water
 from a saucer, and takes his daily specks
 of seed from the candlestick-cup bird
feeder." No one tries to catch—or cage!—him. And we don't *see* him fly
 from place to place. He disappears in a streak,
 blue-tinged column flashed

                on the air. Reappears—above,
        below, in the next room. A firefly's quick-change
nerve pulse, wedded to the dragonfly's long delicate transparent wings:
                I would like to cup my hands around
                his peacock-shiny varicolored head,
    but I am left scooping pockets of vacant space, hollows. . . .
                We're seated in the innermost atrium,
                one of three round tables arranged
in a triangle: speech dialects, buzzing in the air overhead, crisscross
            and mingle in our ears. We discern French patois
                    larded with African slang

                and colloquialisms. Native
        food we order, likewise, is hybrid French creole
cuisine garnished with Afro-herbs and spices: baked fillet of grouper
                thickly sopped in tomato and onion
                marinade; white yam slices, yellow
    breadfruit wedges (pineapple shapes, but soft-textured mush
                like boiled potatoes)—all dishes
                medium priced. . . No meat heavier
than fish or chicken, the anodyne of health foods and the purer mind
        flows in our talk: food of the higher thought,
                food for the Soul's fast. . . .

                    *   *   *

                Do I know *Rastas,* you ask?
        "The *Ganja* pushers?" I reply. "*Dreadlocks* and double
bounce in their walks: men like souped-up hotrods with heavy-duty shocks,
            wide tires and upraised rears?"
                "No! Streetcorner hopheads. They give
        the true *roots* movement a bad name. A whole body of symbol
                and image poetry in our style of walk,
                dress, speech, breathing, music
and dance. It is rhythm. It is tempo. It is faith hatched in the rumble,
        or rattle, of Marley's Reggae chants—his sounds
                our cue! They dredge up

                Rebel Soul to fight
        the oppressor. He's the Carib Bob Dylan, summons
the roots passion of the common folk to rise up against dictators, Juntas—

in all fledgling Carib nations. Black
politics. Black theology. Black roots
economics. A mind passion sweeping the West Indies, and beyond,
a worldwide Black mind esthetic spread
on the limitless wings of Reggae songs,
Reggae dance." "Less Bob Dylan to me," I say, "than the Soul's Gorilla-cry
brute grumble, gains wrung from *Dread* contained,
and primitive Gut-shrieks

of the early Stones' songs,
or today's Punk Rock nose-thumbings at conventions
in dress, gesture, and speech." "Yes and no," you snarl. "It's a question
of history. Public Record. Rasta born
in Jamaica in the Thirties, two full
generations before Rock. In the Seventies, it spread to Carib
newly-founded free nations, *Dread*
a Godchild of the demise of colonial
empires." "But Sparrow and Calypsonians still command a following, yes?"
"Ah! Calypso, songs of woman and sex and carnival,
ran its course from the mid-

Fifties to the mid-Sixties.
Now my father and his cronies still get their kicks,
in secret, from those decadent vaudeville jesters. Reggae's serious man's
Credo. The new wave of artist-exiles,
degrees or career diplomas earned,
come home to rebuild this Island . . ." Poems and prose vignettes
and political broadsides are spread
on the tabletop, one poem's corners
smudged with creole tomato sauce. A color proper to those vituperative
and stormy propaganda leaflets, we agree—our rare
moment of smiling Oneness.

SUNDAY: MY THROAT AFIRE

(Castries, St. Lucia)

Sunday. My throat
afire. All public pharmacies bolted
shut. . . . A local child,
decked out in bright greens—the parish school
uniform—routes me down a wavery path through woods
to the country store. I lose
the pathway twice for tall weeds, spillover thickets,
fallen logs,
and nearly collide with a vine-crisscrossed
wall. *Another door,*
double-boarded over. I turn, thinking to reverse my steps, and pick

my way back
to the main road—but I halt. Overhead,
a voice offers help,
help for all troubles. A tread of sandaled feet—
upon the roof—pads near. "It's my throat," I'm saying.
My finger points to the faulty
organ: "It's nothing, a trifle. Cough drops, any flavor
or brand, will do,
please." But the voice slides over the edges
of my last few words,
neutering their drift: so much devalued currency, out-of-date coin,

cancelled checks.
Shaman or necromancer, voice oily
and unctuous, his tone
is an odd blend of stock-broker and bookie.
Shop closed on Sunday. He and a handyman on the roof
for repairs, or remodelling.
He signals his co-roofer to rest until his return, leaps
down the ladder
(dropping three or four steps at a lunge),
the while he counsels me
on the hidden "infestations, a pestilence" lurking behind common

throat ailments.
"We mustn't just numb de symptoms, y'know.
Gots to stifle de roots!"
He unbuttons his lightweight silk jacket, pokes
two fingers in each of six small vest pockets hand-sewn
in vertical rows: he searches,
distractedly, for a small parcel lost amidst the scramble
of tinkly metals—
keys, coin, nails, pocket clippers, medicine
vial?—with each flick
of his rummaging fingers, he tags and inventories a familiar

stockpile of dopes
and remedies. The smirk of known finds,
undoubted cure-alls, curls
the corners of his mouth as he retracts his hand
from the bottommost slim pocket, a square yellow packet
pinched between thumb and index finger.
The sealed paper sack is frayed, brown-stained at the corners.
"Liver salts,"
he enunciates, as one who chants
Medical Latin, and hands
me the pouch: "Very strong. Potent. In its most concentrated pure

form. Just a pinch
of this powder, mixed with water, kills
de pain. You must gargle,
at intervals..." He groans a sample of Afro-
Gargle, a passable—if wobbly—baritone aria. But first,
his treatment: a surgical tactic,
the prime guarded secret of his pharmacological clan (six
generations
of his family's practise of paramedics'
and drugstore expertise), drawn
from his private store of homecrafts—"herbal arts." He rattles off

polysyllabic
names! Instruments, natural medicines,
elixirs, herbs, potions—
he might be an Austrian Count, or Duke, who boasts

of matchless casks in his private wine cellar. . . . We enter,
stooped, the low doorway of a thatched-palm
hut, iglooshaped, half-darkened. He seats me on a tall stool,
snapping the chain
under the one bare electric bulb, dangled
directly over my eyes,
blinding at first. Then he mutters, by turns, odd magic stigmata

of my disease
and arcane techniques of primitive
crypto-surgery he, alone,
in the Antilles Island Chain is wholly certified
to perform for their cure. . . . I rise to my feet, opposed
by a firm hand pressing me floorward,
the low ceiling bonking my scalp. "The gargle will cure me,"
I feebly protest,
trying to shuffle past him to the door, he
a pillar, immovable guard. . .
He croons a song of my lethal symptoms, never glancing in my throat,

which he proclaims
is "torrid with rawness," "an inflammation,
or conflagration, of the glands
and tonsils." I'm waiting out his prattle, my eyes
now accustomed to the glare of the one bright bulb halfway
lighting the dim cluttered recesses
of the squalid infirmary hut: soiled sheets and bedclothes
in one corner,
cobweb tatters netting the neglected linens;
along one wall, a zigzag row
of assorted bottles, packages, surgical tools—and most striking,

I can just make out
a series of objects suspended by a wire
affixed to the ceiling.
Scanning from roof to floor, I note a hodgepodge
of amulets, charms, bones (rabbit's foot, monkey's paw,
whatnot?), a stained pair of decrepit
cracked old shoes at the bottom, an anchor, a few inches
above the floor—

the chain of talismans, or fetishes, shaken
by winds outside the hut,
the whole thatched dwelling asway, from time to time, in the midday

gusts. . . . My attention
riveted to this display of obeah gewgaws
and gimcrackery, I ignore
my host's pacings from side to side, and his arming
himself—to my sudden alarm—with Q-tips and large cotton
swabs! In one hand, a bottle of amber
liniment; in the other, as he bends near, bidding me
to drop my head
back and "open wide," I see a scalpel's
part-hidden sharp edge flash
between two balls of cotton (wedged tight, so to conceal a weapon). . . .

His handyman
slinks behind him now, both guerillas wrapped
in soiled aprons—the semblance
of surgical gowns, complete with ill-fitting rubber
gloves and gauze face masks. The hunched assistant's figure
is blurred, his hands slyly concealed
behind his boss's shoulders. But he carries bulky implements,
so I surmise,
observing the long shadows of his hands
and their tall contents
cast on the hut wall, a bluish flame flickering from one! A bunsen

burner, or blowtorch?
The head Shaman steps forward, hands poised
to commence glum surgery. . .
I'm up from the stool, scamper out the low-roofed
portal at a single bound: "No hospital Emergency Room
stunts for me," I clown, my terror
no less urgent for the guise of farce. A rubberized claw
snatches, deftly,
the prescribed liver salts from my limp
hand. The masked gargoyle squeals—
in a voice at once testy and hysteric—"I'm finished with you. . . ."

PARLOR SHIP GALLERY

    A SHORT JAUNT down the shore
from Halcyon Sands Hotel—I find myself blankbrained
on her private beach, rap on the patio door, and step inside.
I'm indoors and outdoors at once! So many
of the free form stone sculptures—
partitions between rooms,
    rock piles buttressing the trilevel
staircase—seem modelled from chunks
    of natural breakwater shore rocks: or *gouged,*

    intact, from coastlines I passed
moments before. The pitch and tilt of angled windows,
blent so well with views of inrushing surf, the very house sways,
the kitchen bobbing in wind and waves like the prow
of a great wide-bodied yacht; while forced
domestic incursions
    of sea leap from the actual walls
just past the low-ceilinged
    front foyer. A row of ships, arranged smaller

    to larger, highlights the picture
gallery: the vessels' keels knife through high and low
sea levels, which clash with the outdoors waterline. I must blink
the true horizon—glimpsed through windows—back
in place, while I scan the dream seas
subdivided by borders
    of picture frames lining the lengthy wall
of a living room ship pageant.
    I am led by Madame Choiseul, portrait by portrait,

    through this homemade museum
exhibit of stages in her French-aristocrat husband's
career and shipping empire. A poor youth despite noble family
heritage. *Creme de la creme.* Pristine upper class,
since early seventeen hundreds
(an era of French home
    rule, rare French sovereignty of the Island)...

Photos of the aging shipbuilder
        are hung, in separate silver-tinted small frames,

      beside each vessel. The smaller
wood-hulled ships inaugurate the thirty-five year
saga: exposed boats, sail or oarsman propelled; the early fleet
employed, alternately, for fishing and shipping
according to the season's need.
Later steel-hulled liners
       (growing longer and more streamlined
each year, like the early Sixties'
        tailfin fad in U. S. Cadillacs) relinquished

     local fishing rights to small craft.
Monsieur Choiseul, onetime ship architect, now exporter
Czar, is pictured—at each advanced age—posed before that year's
premiere vessel, his beard newly trimmed, his stance
altered for each ship christening.
Grey tints and speckles
       in his hair and sideburns flower, yearly,
into whorls and streaks. The display
        of photos suggests, by turns, a sportsman—game hunter

      or angler—installed, cheerily,
next to enlarging trophies of the hunt. Or a surreal
concubinage. A litany of matings between man and ship, each pair
of photos a marriage portrait, the applauding crews
all male wedding parties, their numbers—
on deck, or lined up
       on the dock parallel to the ship's flank—
doubled and redoubled, from decade
        to decade. . . . My guide through this life as plaque-

      certified legend, Madame Choiseul,
a ponytailed redhaired mother of three college-age
roués, is plucky Irish! Alain, her eldest and most settled,
home for summer break from Penn State. . . . *Father
and first son appear in the patio
door, at once: long,*
       *loose-muscled men of high breeding,
the older a bit slouched; this pair,*
        instantly spotted to be regal, stallionesque. . . .

THE QUEEN'S LAST FITTINGS

The bare steel frame, to begin, measures thirteen feet
   nine inches tall, twelve feet wide.
      Arrow-tipped, featherlike projections
         will extend high
            between the garage roof joists,
         scraping low rafters
         (the two wide GM cars, parked
in the driveway, require less floor space). . . .
      Seven sons and two daughters
            must be carted to that one roomiest
         two-car garage, donated by friends for construction
            and hideaway storage
         of her costume. Six angular males squeeze

         into my small Hertz Datsun,
      their long bones wound together like pretzel
         twists in my rearview mirror;
      while eldest son,
            father and two daughters
               cram into their U. S. Chevy frontseat
            (separate wing-and-tail assembly units crowding
               the backseat and trunk, buckled trunk lid
         chained to the back bumper). All eleven
         of us come scrambling out four doors at once, it seems,
      in haste of final touch-up,
         the last alterations and remodellings
         in this five-day-marathon sprint of family co-op
      creation. . . . I stand, allured, in the garage
      doorway, and witness

the squadron of brothers mount seven ladders,
   carrying bulky units,
      rivetting loose parts with rivet guns,
         tying wires,
         sledge-hammering steel bolts;
      they pause to inspect,
         or adjust, moveable segments. . .

I might be viewing a small airport hangar,
   workmen reassembling
      a stripped-down ariplane, following
   repairs or routine tune-up of the craft, each man
      so well synchronized
      with the others, their mutual concert

         of tasks is a skilled ensemble. . . .
      Her hair done up in oversize curler spools,
         wearing patched and tattered jeans,
      the older daughter
            (she the current favorite
               Queen contestant, bookies taking her
            as trend setter for odds in local betting) steps
               forward, at frequent intervals; she climbs
         into her snug-fitting capsule, fastens
         the straps in place, and turns from side to side. Some parts
      of her costume—loosely
         attached as yet—are suspended by wires
         or ropes from the garage ceiling, prior to final snips
      of trimming. She loves to model her near-complete
      royal garb, again

and again; each test run reveals flaws, tag ends,
   for modification. As her costume
      approaches its ideal form, her stance
         and deportment
         mellow, her face grown austere.
      Intangibly, she
      and her elaborately wrought
garment seem to alter each other—they interact,
   slowly conceive the miracle
      of queenly beauty, while she passes
         through quick stages from role to identity: a Queen!
         Still again, she lingers
            for long moments, at rest in her carapace,

            or cocoon. I fancy her a human
         caterpillar pupa slowly incubating—she grows
            and matures, one day to burgeon,

                    hatching from her thin
                         membrane of sheathe. But today,
                      she waits, seethes with ripening, arms
                       folded over her breasts, shoulders slumped. She poses
                      for last fittings, the sculptural tailorship
               of that matchless team of costumiers—
                 her father and brothers, catching fire from the hellion swing
            of her hips, the awesome
                  shadows under her cheekbones. They refashion
                    the draperies of silk ribbons and silk embroideries,
      sash and scarf shapes wound about concealed bones
      of that welded steel

skeleton, those intricate steel underpinnings. . . .
    They revere her willowy back,
       divinities of her shoulders, the tilt
          of her neck,
          the swellings of her collar
      bones, her jawbone.
      At some moments, the pitch
     of intensity in the dank garage effervesces,
         the brothers arching their arms
                  and craning their necks forward to the task
            in a pantomime of love holds, a charade of veiled
                embraces. The room
             sizzles with a body heat that could ignite

                   the scattered newspapers and wisps
            of hay, starting a fierce two-car-garage inferno.
                 Spontaneous combustion! . . . Now
         the full burden
                of apparatus is eased,
                   gently, upon her neck and shoulders,
                  a partial helmet shifting some of the dead weight
                 to the back of her head. Her father,
      for an instant, looks grim: "Too heavy?"
      he asks. But she has lift and bounce in her carriage, to spare,
         and she follows his cues,
              a drillmaster leading his pupil through march
              routines—the basic steps of stage promenade, short hops

and pirouettes. The pulleys are reversed. One by one,
   the suspension ropes

and guidewires are released—at last, she navigates
   her full ambulatory throne
      from side to side, traversing the makeshift
         circular stage:
         a small raised platform of plywood
      boards piled, in layers,
   upon the garage floor. Her seven brothers, at ease
      on their various ladder rungs,
            seem amazed by her perky moves, as am I!
         Buoyant slides. Pivots. She whirls to the platform's
            front edge, spreads her arms,
            and I fear she will flap those side panels

               like wings, and lift off. . . She swishes
         with lighter and lighter tread, she and the costume
            blent into the one body,
         as a face grows
               to fit the mask. She's twinned,
                  mated to the marvelous flying machine
               of costume she transports, which her brothers crafted
                  from tubes of steel and scraps of silk fabric
            in five days of steadfast tailoring
            and homecrafts carpentry. It's a cross between a steel-ribbed,
         silk-laced kite, a mammoth
            butterfly, and a hang glider apparatus
            (if wingless, tailless, rudderless). With each balletic turn
and turn about, she is finding her royal gait, knight
in her silken armour. . . .

THE BANANA MADONNA

En route to Roseau
Valley Church, we pass defunct
sugar mills, a few
kept up as *ruins*—followed by lush crops
of banana trees and coconut palms, both casting much shade
and cooling our passage through St. Lucia's
rolling pastures. (Banana images, profuse in local Church
Art, glut our talk)....
Never have I seen so many unpicked bananas at once—
this plantation the richest,
so near to harvest: the thousands of green firm tubes wrapped
in bundles, thousands
of green hands upon hands upon hands—
fingers woven together, wound
about the stalks and vines.... It's the great *Siesta*
of banana trees! The proliferant orchards
doze, Pater and Mater Familias Banana sleeping the long repose
of blessed hands crossed in their laps, crossed
over ample bellies,
green fingers interlocked. *Sleep. The sleep
of bananas*

*toward harvest, while the sun's slow yellow light seeps,
dilutes the vine-tough green of rinds. I dream
the slow quiet goldening of the crops....*
We leave behind the last plantation, bear right
down an elegant short cobblestone side road: "Here, stop!"

The church's brick
face leaps in front of my hood—
before the road gives
any sign of quitting. Our engine idling,
we step from the car. My eye follows golden loops in the jigsaw
pattern of stained-glass panelling
in the tall windows raised above our windshield:
two bright haloes
highlight the upper panes, many panels of varied colors

                        fitted into a composite
design below. Your arms, shaping coils and parabolas in the air
                        over our heads,
       guide my view from the halo above the mahogany
             haired woman's forehead locks
to the marvelous flowing banana forms, arched like horseshoes,
               boomerangs, erect phalluses—
but always, the banana is the norm all bold variations branch
         away from, or return to. Likewise, the borders
                 and outer fragments
           of stained-glass mosaic are all banana
                 twists. They begin

       outside the portrait's visible outline, but undulate
         deep into the midsection of the tableau.
          Other banana twirls and prongs,
    snaking around margins of the painting, appear
to flow into the banana orchards in neighbor plantations,

               the lines of crops
      we'd just passed in our Datsun repeated
          in the crisscrossing color veins
     of glass—banana shapes not merely copied,
but transplanted. . . . Ivy, climbing the church's walls and sending
       forked twin vines across nearby fields,
  blends nature and wall no more seamlessly than stained-
              glass banana designs
   which intertwine the faces and necks of mother
         and child suckling her breast.
Strings of half-peeled bananas swirl into the mother's neck-veins,
               her breast-veins.
     The child, perhaps, imbibes banana milk;
        while mother and child, alike,
inhale banana-flavored air: "She is my Banana Madonna!"
      you are saying. And yes, faces and busts
of baby, Madonna, seem a tapestry woven of banana vines, half-open
   banana peels. Silhouettes of bulky unpeeled bananas,
             winding around frames
   of glass panels, overspill their outlines. . . .
              Banana curves

*and loops flow into curlicues that become the mother's
ear lobe, her dimpled chin, long slanted neck,
the baby's puffed cheek: bananas the leaf,
stem, root; Madonna and child the blossom—ripe fruit
of stained glass to be plucked by the Congregation's Eye.*

V. The Mural of Wakeful Sleep

for Dunstan and Derek

Quattrocento put in paint
On backgrounds for a God or Saint
Gardens where a soul's at ease;
Where everything that meets the eye,
Flowers and grass and cloudless sky,
Resemble forms that are or seem
When sleepers wake and yet still dream. . . .

—W. B. Yeats

I.

DESPITE THE DARKENED
pews and cloisters, I see—at once—
Roseau Church is deep,
spacious. You hasten to the interior
(having seated me in a rear pew bench), throwing open each set
of barred shutters in succession.... Great columns
of daylight come hurtling into the hall with the force
of physical bodies—
hurled masses of light, fierce locomotives of fire—
pouring through the window
gaps. You advance to the front chapel, taking long strides. My stare
overleaps
your imperially tall, slim frame and connects
with the immense altar mural
behind the low stage. The mural ascends to the chapel
roof, fills the entire front wall,
the stage pedestal as wide as the whole church.... The human figures
so lifelike and proportioned, a parishioner
must forget the mountainous
breadth of the bodies, the faces luminous
with a light

that baffles the eye. *How can mere pigment, slapped*
on a brick wall, simulate the color of flesh
vivid with passion of work's holy
instant—or love's, play's, music's? Size eludes
beholders of the whole wall at once. Eyesight flits

from corner to corner,
from midpoint to outermost borders
(which neither terminate
nor frame the scenes, so much as flow
outwards into the life bristling on the far side of Church walls)....
As moviegoers forget the sheer giantism
of human images flickering upon technicolor screens,
stunned, say, by puny
usher chasing a child across the theatre stage, both

fleshly smaller-than-life
townsfolk tiny enough to be hidden in the pants-cuff of silver screen
newspaper Mogul;
or in the pencil case of his Ace heroine
reporter—so I, today,
gasp at the optical incongruity of your six-foot-six
gangling figure, insectlike, poised
on tiptoe in front of the mural, a praying mantis silhouette (I can't
make out your features in the dim
stage-shadowy glimmers,
only your long slim skeletal outline),
italicized,

highlighted on the brilliant colors of mural backdrop.
But no, the painted wall is all foreground, scenes
and players lit from within by the gouache
gum shine of your passion; though your own body,
waving and pointing to *this* musical performer, to *that* steel-

helmeted construction
crewman perched in his cab cage
and leaning forward
to shift the long-handled controls,
is *incorporeal* in this light. Your noble physique pales. *A film*
of cobweb? A wisp of gauze netting?
Diaphanous, in the outstretched stance of a lean electric
short-trim-bearded
hauntingly lovely black man, wafted across the altar
pedestal as if blown,
gently, by trade winds passing through the wide unshuttered windows
cross-ventilating
the Great Hall. You are shouting the names
of sainted and common folk,
alike, blurting short pithy captions under each figure,
sharing anecdotal secrets from your life
that fed the townspeople of your dream fresco—tales of your family
and domestic setting, rumor or gossip
reported of neighbor
village tilted for disguise, yet mirrored
in dream

pictures they nourished. Now you bend forward at the waist,
and I must stand up tall on my low pew bench to follow
your graceful hand tracings of action scenes
in the mural's bottom quadrants. Half-stooped, you wave
your pipe cleaner arms, prancing to and fro. Wide sideways dashes

of antelope or gazelle!
But your matchstick-doll-torso (*Man
the Creator who unwound
the whole Glory Cosmos of wall mural
from the spool of his earth dweller's fantasy*) is narrower of girth
than the Christ Child's rattle, shorter
than the baby's little finger curled around its handle;
your whole grizzled head
smaller than the O of Mary's fondly cooing pursed lips...
*And I know a moment
of terror! You may be swallowed up by a mouth of your own creation,
or lifted
and crushed by infant fingers.* You grow
dimmer in the fading light.
Your skin ashen, your faded denim suit looks ghostly,
illusive, almost *gaseous*, as compared
to the opaque whole colors of your life studies—township of mortals
and divinities mingled in a chromatic
pastel blend of kin:
a family of folk Beings and Saints
ashimmer

in the story Saga of the wall. Our own flesh—yours *or* mine—
seems phantasmal, we the copies, the painting Souls
the originals: you the puppeteer's
marionette whirled by the invisible guide wires
of your actors, your models.... And now, seated beside me, you

marvel at your happy
Fate. That avalanche of energy! Providential
gush. The creative furor
which swept you through the absurd commission—
a seven day time limit!—to complete Roseau Church's altar mural
for a token fee, three hundred West Indian

dollars. Hardly enough money to pay for the paint!
("... then, you can pass
the hat." "Yes," I replied. Nothing looks impossible to me.
Just imagine the jams
I get into.) You tucked a pallet bed in the vestry corner, a hot plate
to boil water,
then began blocking out some eight hundred
square feet of church wall
for the vast bucolic, choosing the countryside and outdoors
format—though you worked by candle light
through the whole week, doors and windows bolted shut every minute.
Now I picture you mixing the colors, working
at all hours to bring back
with paint and brush the light of day
you shut out

with heavy wooden shutters. No clocks. And no sun to tell you
it was time to rest, short naps snatched, seated upright
against the back wall (near the pew we shared,
today); you dozed off, briefly, eyes half open, perhaps,
while you studied the design in progress on the wall opposite. . . .

II.

Never sleeping by plan,
or by scheduled intent, it seemed as if
the painting continued
in your sleep. So often you would *come to*,
with a start, amazed to find the bongo drummer's two tandem drums
placed under his hands' blurred thumps
before you remembered fixing the planes for drum tops,
drum bottoms, beneath
the birdlike flutter and flap of the performer's palms—
while you slept, standing,
one arm braced to hold your knobby starved-thin skeleton parallel
to the wall.
What force impelled your arm, wielding
the many-colored brush?
What genius for a local face coursed through your sketch
marks—the few blobs of color? A flash
of Being, a fleeting glimpse of joy or pain, crossed each profile.
The human moment trapped by your brush's
swift magic. . . . The hours,
days, minutes disappeared, swallowed
by moves

of the brush, you balancing on higher and higher ladders,
and finally makeshift scaffolds, patched together
from old picture frames, discarded rope,
wire, and other debris. To daub color, to mark strokes
was all. Food and sleep fell away. *To paint is to draw breath—*

never before your joy
in art so total, as if the paint itself
issued from your bones.
Its source had seemed the many small bones
in your wrists, your ankles, and the ladder-rung-bruised metatarsals
of your pained foot arches. Smallest bones,
in your somnambulist fantasy, liquefied—one by one—
to yield more paint,
more paint, turning to sainted flesh (you'd recalled

poring over the skeletons
pictured in Medical Anatomies, a boy held spellbound for unnumbered
hours by magic
intertwinings of the many, many tiny bones
in the articulations of ankle,
wrist, foot instep. . .) In your slow martyrdom of self-
dismemberment, first you proffered wrist bones:
perfectly lubricated small bulbs, metacarpal by sliding metacarpal,
melted down to illuminate and golden
the paint. . . . This moment,
seated by my side, you speak of your slow
starvation,

and I seem to behold the small bones of your bare ankles,
bare wrists, shining with inner light. *They glow
again. They are lit embers. Gold coals.
They ache with the twin tasks of lifting the brush
from pail to wall, pail to wall; and lifting your weary hips

from rung to ladder rung,
a rank pain that throbbed and deepened,
in time, as nails pounded—
slowly—into hands, into ankles, must deepen*
(though neither of us speaks of Christ, neither mutters the words,
"crucify, crucify thin bones into paint,"
we both trace images of the Cross disguised—here
and there and everywhere—
in the mural's portraiture). . . . Toward week's end,
so many times a day,
the pounding at the church door began: your wife, daughters, sons,
each howling
to you to come fetch the tray of food
they'd left for you;
complaints growing louder, if you hadn't touched
the last meal. But you opened the door
for no Soul—not wife or child. Food disappeared, from time to time,
but they must not stay, none be present.
You could be dying,
or mortally hurt from a fall, perhaps,
death plunge

from the odd towers of rudely assembled ladders, scaffolds.
They could see segments, wobbly and tilted off-center,
through peepholes in the closed shutters.
But if ever they stopped their strident voices for long
enough to listen, they heard you singing. Ah, you sang and sang

as you worked, finding tunes
and lyrics to match the elation you felt,
pouring your happy melodies
into the broad expanse of wall. For each idea
your hand daubed, others tumbled forth, redoubled. Your brushes
sped up. They raced the welter of images
taking fire in your eye, no way for hand or paint
to stem the unslowable
tide of mental pictures, rushing too fast, too fast,
shaking you on the ladder:
those vibrations set up, your bone bag swung one way, ladder assembly
the other.
Amazing to hear of it, this rabid ladder dance
of a new art scale come
to birth! How lucky the wall itself didn't collapse,
some vibration cycles known to shatter
glass, crystal, forged iron... But you never lost your footing!
And the ladders absorbed your wildest
oscillations and bends,
while you sang of the Soul we imbibe
through paint.

Oh, we can lip paint soul, tongue paint, throat paint, sex paint...
Brain-sing paint soul! Finger and toe, palm and heel—all
touch zones blaze, aquiver with new paint life.
You kept your balance, and often, it seemed, the wall swayed
in time with the swathes of your brush, shifting its angle to catch

a revolving elbow's thrust
when you slipped; or softened to a cushion
for your lolled forehead
when you dozed, by fits and starts, still erect
on your ladder tops. Words of your song you forget, but your theme—
which roared in your blood and drummed

in your temples—found its dual outlets in your throat's
improvised melodies
and the mural's painted figures. You recite for me, now,
amidst scattered verbal
marginalia on the tableau's well springs: "Oh, people are running away
from painting.
I must, somehow, bring back *the world trend*
of painting." And last, your passion
to teach paint joy to children: "It must be Islandwide!
I won't have programs for elite schools, only.
I'll train art teachers, myself. No one else can motivate as I can.
The trick is, we can outwit death with colors!
Just give the children paint
and palette, twelve bright solid whole colors.
Then, step

back!" Your only pedagogic command: "Be free with color...."
You resume the running fact sheet of glosses, oral
footnotes, on the mural's life sources. *Joseph,
Mary, and the Christ Child are Black, you an apostle
of Black Theology—profiled in leading West Indies Journals.*

III.

Joseph's regal forehead,
his high wide cheek bones and jaguarlike
forward pitch of the shoulders,
were modelled after an American basketball player
featured on the cover of *Ebony* magazine—his gaunt carriage risen
to the topmost limit of his highjump
while he executed a flawless *dunk* shot. His head was poised
just under the cover photo
metal net-hoop, transfigured, here, to a gold stark halo
levitated over his creased brow, his bare
upper body now darkly garbed. He becomes the mural's caped Guardian
Angel! His arms,
upraised, encircle holy mother and child—
a caretaker's pose;
while his glittering eyes project beams of light
across outlands of populous muralscape,
a human lighthouse or watchtower. The many folds of his voluminous
cape and undergown billow, as if windswept.
On either flank, his expanded
velours, a furrowing of the robe draperies,
suggest wings

hinted beneath the fabric, seraphic wing plumes braced
for imminent flight, his shoulder muscles rippled,
neck veins inflated with happy passion.
But the Madonna, curled in a round-shouldered
slouch, the baby suckling her breast, exhales icy serenity:

her face, waxen and impassive,
but lovely in its mythic proportions—
marbled purity of feature—
was fashioned from a West African mask
of the Earth Mother you'd copied from a museum rental collection
of anonymous works, a travelling art show
hired by several Windward Island nations, in succession,
funds raised by joint
campaigns of science foundations and art councils. The art

      and science museum curators,
  after heated debate, took turns with the exhibits—works of genius
        and nobility
    displayed with amazingly diverse captions
     while rotated from one museum
  to the other. But you, laughingly, report: "Not one *expert*,
    amongst those art critics of either faction,
who haggled, month after month, for custody of the leased treasures—
   not one, I say, who claimed to know the totemic
      cast of features in each mask
    as well as their very own son's or daughter's
        telltale

  face contours, recognized the true source of my Madonna;
  so startled were they—one and all—by joy I breathed
    into Black Joseph, Black Mary; by my rage
   to rescue our Faith from its theology of death
and morbidity, to translate the Holy Beings into my Vision

      of happy, happy earthiness!"
   You smile, ardent to recount for me the random
      finds that served as models
  to your high fellowship of citizens and immortals.
Often, surprises in divulging your sources seem to brighten your eyes.
   "Look again," you say, pointing to the central
  tableau: "Man, woman and child are woven in a semiabstract
       tapestry of capsules,
  lines of face bones and shoulder muscles of the three figures
      laced with geometric
ornamentation. But despite the detailed overlay of linework, filigree
       of caricature,
    these Holy Ones partake of the blooded life
     of nature and the common man
  spinning around them in the dozens of portraits and scenes
    in peripheral sectors of wall." And I agree!
They both nourish, and take fire from, action scenes encircling them.
   Columnar lines and parallel bars—generated
      by the cubist perspective
  of the oval centerpiece—pass outward, ribboning,
       but they fade

into that naturalistic gallery of townsfolk. At bottom
center, guiding my eye slowly clockwise, you chortle
loud burly affection for the helmeted men
driving derricks, cat tractors, bulldozers: all chug-a-lug
beer-guzzling pals of yesteryear (at age fifty, two years back,

you'd vowed to renounce booze—
too much work slowdown). The reggae dancers
in one corner, bongo drummers
and calypsonian duet in the other, I follow
the eerily visible wave rumble lines of the drummers upwards. We settle
on masked dancers of a troop in carnival
costumes, one harlequin clown midway in a backwards
somersault, his oval pants-seat
marking a perfect bull's eye through the hoop formed
by his mates' four curved arms
joined at the wrists, suspended above his upwards-floating boot heels.
A musician
is rattling the percussive chac-chac beans
shaken in a long metal tube.
Both arms vigorously wield the instrument, while he,
too, appears to dance in high leaps,
one bent knee upraised against his chest, his lips wide with howls
directed, perhaps, at the boy in the uppermost
right corner, bare-chested,
who blows the horn of his queen conch shell.
A dour song

*to the harbor dawn? Or bitter dirge to his sunken heart, love
stolen, his moans safely muffled from the public ear,
and the all-night masquerade?* His solitude
not quite perfect, the song to himself carries to a seated
fisherman behind him, slumped in fog (but *we* can pierce that veil

of mist), hand cupping his ear:
who strains to listen for mourned laments
of the conch, nearly motionless
in his square sailed hand-carved cottonwood
dugout. So still is his boat upon the unrippled sheen of the bay,
so slack the one sleeping canvas drooped

from his slim mast, so well shall he keep the distraught
lover's conch-blown secret.
The lone shore birds cheep and scribble their thin-toed
cuneiform scrawl on the sand. . . .
The softer music of the conch caps the mural's roof-high gold border,
which mutes
the raucous jabber of the calypso singers
and the chac-chac's unstoppable
sputter. By like diminishment, the blurred contortions
of the dance troop are becalmed by the woman
seated overhead, bent forward on her knees, hands pressed together,
fingerends pointed upwards in prayer, asway
from side to side, face lifted
toward a sunrise at sea. *Her least motions*
a sedate dance,

her dress is all of the sun. She amply fills the upper left mural
corner, wide gold head kerchief bulky—but evenly balanced—
over her gold-on-gold embossed lacework dress.
Gold necklaces and bracelets. Gold earrings. Her jewels displayed
in secret sun worship, this priestess of daybreak is the mural's fulcrum!

Laurence Lieberman's work has been widely anthologized; his poems and critical essays have appeared in most of the country's leading magazines—*The New Yorker*, *American Poetry Review*, *The Hudson Review*, *The Kenyon Review*, and *Sewanee Review* among them. The poetry editor for the University of Illinois Press and professor of English at the University of Illinois, he is the author of four previous books of poetry, *The Unblinding* (1968), *The Osprey Suicides* (1973), *God's Measurements* (1980), and *Eros at the World Kite Pageant* (1983), as well as a collection of essays on contemporary poets, *Unassigned Frequencies: American Poetry in Review* (1977).